Klezmer

Hankus Netsky

Klezmer

Music and Community in
Twentieth-Century Jewish Philadelphia

TEMPLE UNIVERSITY PRESS
Philadelphia • Rome • Tokyo

TEMPLE UNIVERSITY PRESS
Philadelphia, Pennsylvania 19122
www.temple.edu/tempress

All reasonable attempts were made to locate the copyright holder for the cover illustration. If you believe you are the copyright holder, please contact Temple University Press, and the publisher will include appropriate acknowledgment in subsequent editions of the book.

Library of Congress Cataloging-in-Publication Data

Netsky, Hankus, author.
   Klezmer : music and community in twentieth-century Jewish Philadelphia /
Hankus Netsky.
       pages cm
   Includes bibliographical references and index.
   ISBN 978-1-4399-0903-4 (cloth : alk. paper) — ISBN 978-1-4399-0905-8 (e-book)
1. Klezmer music—Pennsylvania—Philadelphia—20th century—History and criticism.
2. Jewish musicians—Pennsylvania—Philadelphia—20th century—History and criticism.
3. Jews—Pennsylvania—Philadelphia—Music—History and criticism.   4. Klezmer
music—Social aspects—Pennsylvania—Philadelphia—History—20th century.   I. Title.
   ML3528.8.N48 2015
   781.62'924074811—dc23

                                                                2014048496

ISBN 978-1-4399-0904-1 (paper : alk. paper)

♾ The paper used in this publication meets the requirements of the American National Standard for Information Sciences—Permanence of Paper for Printed Library Materials, ANSI Z39.48-1992

Printed in the United States of America

9 8 7 6 5 4 3 2 1

Table of Contents

Acknowledgments

I would like to thank my academic mentor and dissertation advisor Mark Slobin for his generosity, patience, camaraderie, and extraordinary guidance, and especially for being the visionary spirit who turned klezmer into an acceptable topic of academic discourse. I am also extremely grateful to Barbara Kirshenblatt-Gimblett and Su Zheng who gave me a tremendous amount of support, encouragement, and help with this project.

This book would not have been possible without my informants, who provided me with music, historical information, anecdotes, encouragement, and lots to think about. I would particularly like to thank Bobby Block, Marvin Katz, Elaine Hoffman Watts, Morris Hoffman, Joe Borock, and Bernie Uhr, all of whom made themselves available whenever I needed information about anything and, when they didn't know the answers, knew exactly where to send me. I would also like to acknowledge the behind-the-scenes help of Minnie Fryer, Josh Waletzky, Lilly Schwartz, Donald Davis, and Michael Elkin, who provided me with contact information for informants whom otherwise would have been inaccessible.

Sholom Altman, Marsha Bryan Edelman, Henry Sapoznik, Jenny Romaine, and Lorin Sklamberg gave me unlimited access to the extraordinary sound archives at Gratz College (Philadelphia) and YIVO (New York). This project also benefited greatly from recordings made available to me by Dr. Samuel Katz, Jack Saul, Alan Shapiro, Alan Bern, Elaine Hoffman Watts, Lev Liberman, Mark Slobin, Herman and Rhoda Hershman, Michael Schlesinger, Jeff Warschauer, Ben Laden, Jack Kessler, Susan Watts, and Bobby Block. Jackie Borock, Elaine Hoffman Watts, Mark Slobin, and Michael Alpert generously supplied me with unique video footage.

I would like to thank Jerry Adler, Kol Katz, Stanley Shupak, Dr. Samuel Katz, Marvin Katz, Jerry Weinstein, Henry Sapoznik, Joe Borock, Elaine Hoffman Watts, Bobby Block, Walter Zev Feldman, Steve Greenman, and the family of Nathan Freedman for allowing me access to the music folios that informed the core substance of chapters 4 and 5.

I would also like to acknowledge the invaluable editing help I received from Franya Berkman, Linda Chase, Beth Brooks, Catherine Johnson, Angela Phillips, Gail Chalew, and especially Angela Piliouras, as well as the indispensible assistance of music copyists Nicolas Urie and Arthur Felluca. Additionally, I would like to thank Micah Kleit of Temple University Press for seeing this project to its conclusion.

I am particularly grateful for the extraordinary support I received from Jackie Borock, without whose collaboration this project would have been much more difficult and not nearly as rich. I would like to thank Hy Goldman and Klezkanada for allowing me to use their extraordinary klezmer workshops as laboratories for my research and Henry Sapoznik and Sherry Mayrent who, back in 2000 through their "Living Traditions" Klezkamp, gave me free rein to create a week-long Philadelphia klezmer fantasy world. I would also like to thank my wife, Beth Brooks, for her patience and encouragement, especially as the time of completion grew near. And, finally, I would like to dedicate this work to the memory of Jerry Adler, Kol and Samuel Katz, Samuel Feldsher, Freddie Kornfeld, Doris Kandel Rothman, Harry Gorodetzer, Harold Karrabel, Morris Zeft, Jules Helzner, Joe Familant, Bobby Roberts, Jay Jerome, Howie Leess, Max Epstein, Harold Singer, Bobby Roberts, Bernie Uhr, Joe Borock, Morris Hoffman, and especially Jim Becker and my parents, Rhoda and Lester Netsky.

Klezmer

Introduction

There are many ways to uncover the story of a Jewish community. Immigration figures, demographic patterns, minutes of board meetings, fundraising goals, and synagogue enrollments are the usual sources that provide data. These documents tell us, among other things, how many people are in the group being studied, where they came from, how the community has evolved, and what they have accomplished. Experts carefully chronicle the progress of religious, political, philanthropic, cultural, and educational institutions, looking for signs of success, stability, cohesion, and deterioration. As traditional historians take stock of the data they gather, they ponder why some institutions remain vital while others outlive their usefulness and either undergo serious renovations or are replaced by new ones that better suit the needs of new generations.

Contemporary historians have broadened the scope of such endeavors. In *The Search for a Usable Jewish Past,* David Roskies (1998) considers the story told by shtetl (Eastern European Jewish small town) literature, Holocaust studies, religious tomes, Yiddish folksongs, Zionist tractates, and the notes of burial societies. Other authors look for clues about Jewish communal history by exploring such subjects as food (Kirshenblatt-Gimblett 1987, Joselit 1994), marriage (Joselit 1994), and sex (Biale 1992). This book draws its historical narrative from a more obscure, but perhaps equally revealing source: the documentary and ethnographic history of professional Jewish musical entertainers (klezmorim) and of the music they performed at Philadelphia's Jewish life-cycle and communal celebrations.

My focus is on the klezmer tradition in Philadelphia over the course of the entire twentieth century, a period stretching from the later part of the Eastern European Jewish immigrant era through the contemporary resurgence of klezmer music.[1] I selected Philadelphia because it is a large and resilient regional American Jewish community with a rich, hitherto mostly uncollected klezmer music legacy[2] and because of my own Philadelphia roots, which, more than any other factor, made this study possible.

Looking at a local klezmer tradition can illuminate connections that are often overlooked in ethnomusicological studies. The issues I address here include the nature of musician cultures (and of the klezmer tradition in particular), the ongoing tension between sacred and secular in music, the complexity of hybrid ethnic musical expression, the insider-outsider dynamic in klezmer, the story told by a single piece of music over time, and the ethnography of a nearly extinct regional musical community. It is really at the intersection of all of these topics that my study takes place, since all are embodied by klezmer, a sacred/secular genre with a long tradition as the music of Jewish communal celebrations and with a recent history as a revitalized concert music played by younger musicians including me.

Located only ninety miles southwest of New York City, Philadelphia boasted a klezmer music culture whose history contrasted starkly with that of its much larger, more diverse, and more trend-setting neighbor. After the upheaval of the post–World War II era, by which time virtually every other community had laid its klezmer tradition to rest, many of Philadelphia's musicians held on to their old-world repertoire, even with the knowledge that they were entirely out of pace with the rest of Jewish society. Indeed, Philadelphia's surprisingly enduring klezmer scene is one of the few that, at the time of my study, still boasted a large enough number of veteran musicians to make a klezmer ethnography worthwhile.

Much of my source material has been gleaned from interviews that I conducted with approximately sixty Jewish wedding musicians, caterers, and descendants of musical families. My research began in 1974, when I embarked on my own quest to explore an avenue of musical expression that had been part of my family's history for at least three generations before I was born.[3]

Charting the history of a klezmer community is not a straightforward task, and at the time I began my research I found very few guideposts. When I proposed writing on klezmer as a project in a multicultural music class during my undergraduate years at the New England Conservatory, I was strongly discouraged. At that time, English-language print sources on klezmer ranged from antiquated to totally erroneous, and I had no idea how to go about finding materials that might support my study.

Nevertheless, I set out on my project, first interviewing elderly members of my own family who had played in Jewish wedding bands in Philadelphia from the 1920s through the 1960s. They provided me with sketchy historical information, lists of additional names, and an assortment of attitudes ranging from enthusiasm to disbelief. They also provided me with a calling card that I could use in approaching other musicians: my "family lineage," essential in a secretive field such as klezmer, in which insider information is routinely kept close to the vest. My often frustrating attempts to conduct klezmer research in other locales have given me cause to appreciate this link more and more as the years go by.

My first "klezmer" contact was my uncle Marvin who had played trumpet in wedding bands from the late 1940s through the mid-1960s. He referred me to my great-uncle, Dr. Samuel Katz, an ex-musician who had given up his cornet and his freewheeling lifestyle in the mid-1930s to start a family and pursue a career in dentistry. Uncle Sam played me recordings of many of klezmer's most important musical figures, including New York–based violinist-bandleader Abe Schwartz and clarinetists Naftule Brandwein, Dave Tarras, and the crotchety, miserly Philadelphia-based Itzikl Kramtweiss, a wild character with whom he had worked on many occasions. He showed me klezmer tune books penned by his first cornet instructor, a transplanted old-world bandmaster named Meyer Swerdlow, and manuscripts of repertoire he had learned from Lou Lemisch, an American-born clarinetist and bandleader who hailed from one of Philadelphia's oldest klezmer dynasties. Perhaps most importantly, he told me stories that provided a window into a very different musical and social milieu from any I had known—a tough and unforgiving world, full of treachery, jealousy, and closely guarded family secrets (several of which involved my own family—oy!). It did not take long for me to realize that the rich musical world he was sharing with me could lead me to a deeper understanding of not only my own ancestry (musical and otherwise) but also the entire Jewish immigrant experience.

My success with Uncle Sam convinced me to probe deeper, and to do so, I called on two other surviving musicians whom Sam had identified from an old photograph of my grandfather's band (ca. 1925). Joe Familant, the banjo player, had become a hairdresser; like many klezmorim (professional Jewish folk instrumentalists), he hailed from a family of musicians and barbers. In his suburban New Jersey condominium, I heard about wild Hasidic, Romanian, and gypsy parties and the eclectic repertoire of "Old Man" Dave Finklestein. Since Joe was still playing both ukulele and drums, he also gave me a few basic musical tips.

Morris Hoffman, whom my uncle had erroneously identified in the photo (the clarinetist in the photo was actually a fellow named Johnny Goodman who did look a fair amount like him), immediately pointed out the irony of my call to him. He had originally learned Jewish dance music at his father's knee. His brothers included the virtuoso concert and klezmer percussionist Jacob Hoffman and the Yiddish theater drummer Johnny Hoffman. But Morris's career had followed a typically American progression, from ethnic roots to mainstream versatility. At the time I contacted him, he was still playing six nights each week at the Latin Casino, a popular Philadelphia nightclub where he had held one of the band's woodwind chairs since the day the club had opened in 1949. "Let me get this straight," he said. "You're nineteen years old and you want to learn about klezmer music? Well, I don't really play it anymore; tonight I'm playing for the Four Temptations [sic],[4] and tomorrow I'll be backing the Supremes" (M. Hoffman 1978).

At my grandmother's suggestion, I visited the musicians' union, still on Eighteenth Street near Arch at the time. The hall was quite the relic, like a saloon in an old western town; I could only imagine the card games and conversations that had gone on here over the years. Lou Herman, the union president at the time, was very friendly; he knew all of my relatives and suggested that I contact a few of the old-timers, including bandleader Abe Neff and trumpeter Morris Zeft. At the same time, he could not figure out why I might want to study a music that was such an inconsequential part of contemporary culture.

Calls to various leads that my uncle gave me bore occasional fruit, but it still was not clear to me where all this might lead. One of my other great-uncles, clarinetist Jerry Adler, was particularly bitter and negative. "What could you possibly want with that music?" he said. "It's gone, dead, buried. If you try to play it, you'll starve" (Adler 1976, pers. comm.). A mass of contradictions, Uncle Jerry had eked out his primary living installing Venetian blinds and radiator caps and kept every cent he had ever earned inside his mattress. He played hot and cold with me for years, occasionally punctuating our meetings with recordings of weddings and bar mitzvahs where he had played wailing *freylekhs* (traditional Eastern European Jewish dances) on his Albert-system "C" clarinet.[5] He would never do me the honor of finishing a sentence when I asked him a question, but in the end he gave me his entire music collection, hundreds of tunes that had taken him years to write out. Eventually, I received his message loud and clear: "These are the Dead Sea Scrolls. It's up to you to figure out what they mean."

Unfortunately, my subsequent attempts to contact local musicians led nowhere. Perhaps I called the wrong ones or simply did not know where to begin—or how to explain what I was after, or even how to conduct an interview. Soon, I gave up and began to focus my energy on the music itself, which was mostly available on 78 RPM recordings. I listened to and transcribed many hours of these recordings and eventually began to share what I had learned with my classes at the New England Conservatory in Boston, where I joined the faculty in 1978. It seemed to me that the music had its own intrinsic merits, and I felt vindicated when my students responded positively to it. Around the same time, I became aware that a klezmer revival was underway, with active proponents in Los Angeles, Berkeley, and New York City. Eventually, one of my students (Merryl Goldberg, now an arts education professor at California State University in San Marcos) persuaded me to organize a concert featuring some of the songs and dances I had transcribed. This well-attended performance, which took place in Boston in February 1980, officially launched the Klezmer Conservatory Band and marked the start of my own professional klezmer career.

The klezmer revival had a profound effect on the klezmer scene and even made believers out of members of my family. Prompted by other activists, klezmer icons, including preeminent New York clarinetists Dave Tarras and Max Epstein, came out of retirement, offering their services both as teachers and performers. Henry Sapoznik's Klezkamp spawned numerous offshoots, workshops and camps that have attracted large multigenerational klezmerhungry crowds in the United States and abroad. My own band became relatively well known, making numerous appearances on public radio's "A Prairie Home Companion;" collaborating with actor Robin Williams, Broadway star Joel Grey, and concert violinist Itzhak Perlman; and providing the scores for several high-profile films, ballet and dance performances, and theatrical productions. I was also able to bring the music back to Philadelphia, performing it at synagogues, senior centers, YMHAs, universities, and prestigious concert venues such as the Academy of Music, the Mann Music Center (with violinist Itzhak Perlman), and, eventually, the Kimmel Center.

In 1996, when I turned my focus back to research, I found myself working in a very different climate. No longer considered an obscure, embarrassing, and archaic part of America's Jewish past, klezmer had become a point of departure for some of the world's most creative and enterprising musicians. Its resurgence had attracted the attention of numerous scholars and journalists, and since then, several full-length studies have explored the music's revitalization, including Rogovoy (2000), Slobin (2000, 2002), Ottens and Rubin (2003), Sapoznik (1999), and Strom (2002).

Luckily, the klezmer resurgence also had a positive effect on many of Philadelphia's old-timers (the few that were still alive!), who realized that the music they were once scorned for playing was now considered "interesting" enough to be the subject of a PhD thesis. In this new climate, I found that many of klezmer's more experienced practitioners desperately wanted their story to be told. I worked with producer/filmmaker Jackie Borock and with the Philadelphia Jewish Archives on a film documenting the city's Jewish wedding music scene.[6] Along with veteran clarinetist and saxophonist Joe Borock (Jackie's father), trumpeters Marvin Katz (my uncle) and Susan Watts (Morris Hoffman's grandniece), guitarist/banjoist Barry Warhaftig, bassist Harold Singer, and percussionist Elaine Hoffman Watts (Morris Hoffman's niece), I performed and recorded some of Philadelphia's 1940s klezmer repertoire with a group that I dubbed the Philadelphia Klezmer Heritage Ensemble. I even wrote a monthly newspaper column for Philadelphia's leading Jewish newspaper, the *Jewish Exponent*, titled "Professor Klezmer," trying to raise consciousness about the local Jewish wedding music tradition and hoping to acquire additional data and materials. I can imagine the editor's response had I proposed such a column back in 1974!

The response to all these activities was extraordinary. I received detailed written communications from vocalist Edith Lit—one of the best singers on the traditional Jewish music scene and the wife of Dave Kantor, the last of the truly "greenhorn" bandleaders, from the son of "Singing Jack Orkin," a prominent Jewish drummer and entertainer and from Lou Gold whose brother, Al, had been one of the last Jewish "Cordovox" (electrified accordion) players. I was able to speak in person with Bobby Roberts, Jay Jerome, Jules Helzner, Stu Harris (Hoffman) Harold Rubin, Marty Portnoy, Alan Helzner, Marty Lahr, Bobby Block, and Jackie Gold, all prominent Jewish society bandleaders with strong Jewish roots, as well as with sidemen including Victor Mazer (stage name: Chick

Sherr), Max Spector, Mel Davis, Cal Shaw, Bernie Weinstein, Elliot Jacoby, Freddie Kornfeld, Bernie Greenbaum, and Pat Shalenza. Vocalist Geri Dean became a particularly gracious and generous source, along with well-known Philadelphia-born Hollywood composer Dave Raksin. Family members of old-time bandleaders, veteran caterers and florists, and prominent local klezmer revival figures also opened their doors to me, giving me pretty much everything I needed to pull the pieces back together.

I also began to look into the stories of klezmorim in other cities. My band's travels afforded me the opportunity to compare Philadelphia's klezmer story and repertoire to those of Milwaukee, Detroit, Boston, Baltimore, Chicago, and New York. Doing so convinced me that Philadelphia's klezmer scene was indeed both unique and historically significant.

I must admit that, at various times when I was working on unearthing Philly's klezmer scene, I found myself on slightly uneasy footing as a researcher. As ethnomusicologists are so fond of asking, was I an outsider or an insider? Clearly, by some standards (my uncle Jerry's for example), I would have to be considered an outsider, although at some point I seemed to have become an insider whose musical output has been pivotal, at least to the revival of the genre. I am not alone in this regard. At least six other active performers who were attracted to klezmer while in their late teens or twenties (Joel Rubin, Walter Zev Feldman, Joshua Horowitz, Michael Alpert, Henry Sapoznik, and Yale Strom) have published articles or books on the subject, and I would not be surprised if many more individuals join their ranks in the years ahead. It is perhaps worth considering how this new cadre of "klezmer experts" fits into ethnomusicology in general and the klezmer world in particular.

In *The Study of Ethnomusicology*, Bruno Nettl (1983) cautions "outsider" scholars against representing themselves as or trying to transform themselves into "insider" master musician. He makes it clear that he prefers to leave the teaching of world music to bona-fide insiders (268). Nettl seems to have formed his conservative view of transmission in his early years while studying Persian *dastgah* (an intricate modal tradition) with a teacher who expressed the kind of skepticism that would have made many of my family members proud. "You will never understand this music," he was told in no uncertain terms, after he attempted to chant a passage in traditional style (259). Humbled, Nettl vowed to confine himself to the circumscribed role of theoretical ethnomusicologist. While he might study a style of world music and appreciate the intricacies of its construction, he would never feel comfortable teaching the style himself and spent much of his career cautioning world music students against doing so.

Despite Nettl's warnings, today's ethnomusicology features a wide array of "outsider" scholars who teach *gamelan,* African drumming, north Indian *raga,* and countless other ancient and once far less accessible world music styles with varying degrees of effectiveness and cultural sensitivity. Ethnomusicological study has in many ways mirrored the eclectic ambitions of contemporary classical and popular musicians who liberally borrow from many traditions, ignoring the admonitions of cautious scholars. The lure of world music is too great for many of its adherents to resist, or as Mark Slobin puts it, "The exotic can be much more powerful than the national or the diasporic, since an imaginary connection that fuels the fires of passion can even drive a person to lifelong commitment" (Slobin 2000: 18).

Actually, this phenomenon, which is not uncommon in revivals, is a salient feature of the American folk revival, a movement that arguably made the neo-klezmer phenomenon possible. The folk revival of the 1950s was launched not by mountaineers, but by young New York–based folklore students, only some of whom had southern roots. Groups such as the Kingston Trio "with their colorful short-sleeve Ivy League shirts, close-cropped hair, easy drollery, and unambiguous enthusiasm" (Rosenberg 1993: 45) came to represent the folk culture they ostensibly parodied. As Robert Cantwell points out in his essay "When We Were Good: Class and Culture in the Folk Revival" (included in *Transforming Tradition,* Neil Rosenberg's anthology of essays on music revivals), American folksong revivalists set the stage for later ethnic music revivals:

> They inspired thousands of young middle-class men and women to learn folksongs, to accompany themselves on folk instruments, particularly the guitar and banjo, to search out and lionize authentic folk musicians, and finally to dress, groom, speak, comport themselves and even attempt to think in ways suggestive of the rural, ethnic, proletarian, and other marginal cultures to whom folksong was supposed to belong. In this process, many kinds of music that at other periods had been commercially performed and recorded, such as blues, old-time and bluegrass music—music chiefly of southern or southeastern rural origin—came to be regarded as folk music and enjoyed a revival on that basis, to be followed in the next decade by Irish *ceili,* Klezmer, and other ethnic musics. (Cantwell 1993: 36)

The klezmer world is a perfect place to question the lines between musical insider and outsider, and in truth, I still think it is unclear exactly where the boundaries fall. Yet one thing is certain: Studies of Jewish communal life have generally been done by Jews. In his book, *Between Two Worlds: Ethnographic Essays on American Jewry,* Jack Kugelmass takes note of the likely reason for the often self-reflexive nature of much American Jewish ethnography:

> It does seem rather clear that it is integrally related to the general issue of ethnic identity as an alternative to hegemonic ideologies, or, as Michael Fischer argues in regard to ethnicity, "as alternatives to the melting pot rhetoric of assimilation and to the bland, neutral style of the conformist 1950s." Indeed, the search for that identity is particularly acute within the postmodern world of fragmented cultural universes. In this sense, the personal quest for authenticity and communal identity needs to

compete deep within the heart of the anthropologist with interests that are purely scientific. (Kugelmass 1988: 2)

I would contend that the same argument holds true for Jewish musicians involved in the klezmer revival. The movement fulfills the needs of its proponents on several levels, with its music functioning both as a topic for serious study and as a pathway to personal musical identity. In any event, this has certainly been true for me.

As in all of the revivals mentioned earlier, it did not take long for those revitalizing klezmer to eclipse their mentors in both popularity and financial success. From my insider/outsider position, I cannot help but notice the discrepancy between the high status that was achieved by those who played the retooled music of the neo klezmer movement and the much lower status generally accorded the older generation of Jewish wedding musicians.[7] It is in the context of the klezmer revitalization movement that Barbara Kirshenblatt-Gimblett labeled klezmer a "heritage" music, defining heritage as "a mode of cultural production in the present with recourse to the past," which can add value to a commodity. In her opinion, heritage could not "be lost and found and always remains accessible" (Kirshenblatt-Gimblett 1995: 37).

On further reflection, I have come to realize that Kirshenblatt-Gimblett's definition of heritage had little resonance with the view of klezmer music espoused by many of my informants in the period of my early research (before the "revival"). When I found out about klezmer music, I was promptly told that there was no way for me to learn it. My uncle Jerry articulated this view well: to him, the only way to become a klezmer was to be "born into it." Only now do I understand that being a klezmer was a much larger issue than the simple act of playing the music. If there were no longer dimly lit catering halls, endless family weddings, or dances that degenerated into fistfights, then there was no longer a klezmer tradition to be born into. Even though four of my uncles, my grandfather, and my great-grandfather had all grown up performing the music (providing me with at least enough of a bloodline to do interviews), the torch could not really be passed on to my generation. As a part of a culture that had been both abandoned and destroyed, in Jerry's view, the music would have to rest in peace.

The lesson I learned from Jerry Adler was that an abandoned heritage is not a true heritage at all. Many of the musicians I interviewed had watched klezmer music go from something in vogue to something old-fashioned but serviceable and then to something useful only as the hokiest form of nostalgia. It did not even seem within the realm of possibility that it could be in vogue again or that the culture of my great-uncle's generation would find any resonance with younger performers, and to a large extent those older musicians were right: What we revived bore little resemblance to their culture. For those of the older generation, the neo-klezmer movement was merely a curiosity.

It fell to me and to several other independently motivated activists to create a context in which what we saw as the klezmer heritage (basically, the music itself) could become available again.[8] As new "revival" contexts took hold, klezmer splintered into such diverse communities as mainstream, fusion, downtown, feminist, classical, historical performance, religious, and even "tourist-oriented."[9] Indeed, klezmer did become a "heritage" music,[10] but one might argue that it did so at the expense of its roots.

Of course, the revitalization movement's klezmer is not, to paraphrase some ironic downtown New York hype, "my grandfather's klezmer." While offshoots of the movement (including many trendy hybrid forms) have become well known as far away as Japan and New Zealand, the story of traditional klezmer as performed in American cities has remained shrouded in mystery. Except for the folklorized accounts found in Yiddish fiction, almost nothing has been written on the music and its performers that focuses on its formational performance context—the music of Jewish weddings and celebrations.[11] Even when older performers have been interviewed and quoted, they quickly segue to their careers as recording, radio, and concert musicians[12] to project more "respectable" public personas. Their deliberate obfuscation of their years in the wedding scene has only further fueled my desire to learn the real story.

I had noticed that portrayals of klezmorim in Jewish folklore, including in short stories by Peretz (1947), Rabinovitsh (1979), and Singer (1982), tended to reinforce derogatory and romantic stereotypes, including images of Jewish wedding musicians as itinerants who engage in every possible deviant practice, a conclusion that my research has in many ways corroborated. Yet the idea of musicians' lives as models of deviant behavior is not at all limited to Jewish literature. It is a common theme in African American music history, especially evident in Keil 1966 and explored in detail in *Outsiders* by Howard S. Becker (1963), who studied the culture of club-date musicians in Chicago to obtain his data. He notes that the musicians' culture is built firmly on a dichotomy that, in the language of the 1950s, separated musicians from "squares":

> The musician is conceived of as an artist who possesses a mysterious artistic gift setting him apart from all other people. Possessing this gift, he should be free from control by outsiders who lack it . . . . This attitude is generalized into a feeling that musicians are different from and better than other kinds of people . . . . An extreme of this view is the belief that only musicians are sensitive and unconventional enough to be able to give real sexual satisfaction to a woman . . . . The family . . . as an institution that demands that the musician behave conventionally, creates problems for him of conflicting pressures, loyalties and self-conceptions. His response to these problems has a decisive effect on the duration and direction of his career. (Becker 1963: 85–87)

This attitude is precisely the problem of the klezmer. Within his[13] own world he sees himself as a superior individual with great gifts and extraordinary powers, but within Jewish and general society he is part of the underclass, a legion of what Peter Stallybrass and Alon White call the "low domain." In *The Politics and Poetics of Transgression,* they explore why societies feel the need to define themselves by differentiating between high and low, polite and vulgar, civilized and grotesque and branding those consigned to the lower echelons with an aura of disgust. This is not to deny that society does, in some way, relish what such individuals bring to it:

> But disgust always bears the imprint of desire. These low domains, apparently expelled as "Other," return as the object of nostalgia, longing, and fascination. The forest, the fair, the theatre, the slum, the circus, the seaside resort: all these, placed at the outer limit of civil life, become symbolic contents of bourgeois desire. (Stallybrass and White 1986: 192)

It is not much of a stretch to add the bandstand to this list of venues. Still, according to Stallybrass and White, looking at any type of underclass poses a problem to the academic:

> These contents, or domains, are subject to misrecognition and distortion precisely because idealization and phobic avoidance have systematically informed their discursive history. Thus, on the one hand, these sites have been singled out by some social historians in a nostalgic and privileged way as the ever vanishing trace of real "community." But this precisely duplicates, at the level of academic discourse, the object of analysis. On the other hand, "rigorous theory" has tended to look down upon "mere content" as obvious, crude, and vulgar, redeemable only through a process of abstraction and refinement. (Stallybrass and White 1986: 193)

Perhaps it is this fear of less savory elements that has kept the full story of klezmer and many other aspects of Jewish culture from public view. This may explain why Jewish scholars have also paid relatively little attention to the *bad-khones* (folk poetry) tradition and to the *shund* (popular or, more literally, "trash") Yiddish theater. While some attention has been paid to Jewish folksong, it has mostly come from writers based in sociology or cultural anthropology. Indeed, the prejudice has also been geographic: Jewish historians have always tended to favor the scholarly Jewish heritage of the northern Jewish settlements of Poland and Lithuania over the folk religion and culture of the more southern Ukrainian and Moldavian Jews (Tabak 1990: 4). One must look to fiction for windows into the psyche of Jews from less erudite backgrounds.

The scholarly focus in the field of Jewish music studies has been similarly narrow. An antisecular bias figures prominently in the writings of the pioneering Jewish musicologist, Abraham Zvi Idelsohn, who nevertheless included a well-researched and useful chapter on klezmorim in one of his books. Idelsohn's overall conception of Jewish music was inherently intertwined with Jewish religious society, which he regarded as its only true source. He expressed this viewpoint in his seminal work, *Jewish Music in Its Historical Development:* "Life as the Jew visualized it has no room for what is commonly denominated 'secular,' therefore Jewish folksongs are rooted in the sacred. . . . Sacred song has been folk song and folk song, sacred song. Jewish folk song nestles in the shadow of religion and ethics" (Idelsohn 1929: 358).

There is a lot to be said for this viewpoint. Indeed, many of the signifiers (most important and unique characteristics) of Jewish musical performance might well be linked to religious expression, and in many cases, religious songs have become templates for later secular songs, although the reverse has also been true.

Yet, traditional Jewish music scholarship has also often carried with it a rampant disregard for hybridized diasporic traditions that can be directly traced to Idelsohn's solidly Zionist ideology: "The Jews have never been divorced from the land where they developed from nomadic tribes into a nation. The topography, the atmosphere, the very soil of Palestine, was molded into their faith, their thought, their spiritual culture, and folklore" (Idelsohn 1929: 357).

Other musicologists (Jewish and non-Jewish alike) were quick to accept Idelsohn's obsession with Israel as Jewish music's "wellspring," ignoring the possibility that, given the Jews' thousand-plus years' sojourn in various parts of Europe, other templates might be more relevant. For many years, none questioned his discovery of "timeless unifying principles" in Jewish melody or his tracing of these principles back to "biblical-era" sources. Even today, many Jewish music scholars follow Idelsohn's dicta, downplaying the "Jewishness" of diasporic traditions.[14]

Other Jewish music scholars chose to see the klezmer tradition as a relic embedded deeply in the Jews' distant European past. As recently as 1975, cantorial scholar Macy Nulman, wrote the following: "The klezmer, an itinerant musician fulfilling the artistic and cultural needs of the Jewish community, appeared in Central, Western, and Eastern Europe until about the middle of the nineteenth century" (Nulman 1975: 138–139). He goes on to state that, although itinerant and musically illiterate, klezmorim "were the forerunners of numerous Jewish interpretative musicians (classical violinists and pianists), and important in the development of European art music" (140). By 1929, Idelsohn was already writing about klezmorim in the past tense, as did Amnon Shiloah as recently as 1992. It is as if the emergence of a Jewish art music tradition rendered the klezmer tradition intrinsically obsolete.

The first Jewish ethnomusicologist to squarely challenge the Jewish music scholars' view of klezmer was Moshe Beregovski, head of the ethnomusicological section of the Institute of Jewish Proletarian Culture of the Ukrainian Academy of Sciences from 1930 until it was closed in 1948 (the exact dates are in some dispute). As Mark Slobin writes in the introduction to his translation of a collection of Beregovski's essays and musical transcriptions, "[Beregovski recontextualized] the Jews as a part of a rich inter-ethnic musical network within a given region" (Beregovski 1982: 3). Unlike many Jewish ethnographers who preceded him, Beregovski created his own detailed musical transcriptions, and in contrast to his Jewish music studies predecessors and contemporaries, he was deeply interested in the Jewish informant's entire cross-cultural repertoire. His collecting expeditions in the southern Ukraine led to the publication of several pivotal volumes, first published in Russian in the 1930s and, more recently, translated into English and published in the United States. In this passage from the introduction to his 1934 folksong collection, he takes issue with the more mainstream Jewish music studies approach:

> The zealous adherents and preservers of the liturgical musical tradition condemned Jewish secular folklore to death and did not want to believe that this useless "Yiddish musical jargon" lay at the basis of Jewish "national music culture." The only Jewish music worthy of "regeneration" according to the clerical Zionists (Idelsohn, et al.) was the "lofty liturgical melody." (Beregovski 1982: 22)[15]

Beregovski modeled his work on that of K. V. Kvitka, a Ukrainian ethnomusicologist for whom he had great respect and with whom he worked for many years. He based his methodology on Kvitka's interethnic model for collecting local materials. Beregovski's ideas and research propelled Soviet Jewish ethnomusicology in the direction of documenting the co-territorial sharing of melodies. This concept formed the basis for the subsequent comparative work of a fellow Soviet, scholar Max Goldin, whose pioneering article, "On Musical Connections between Jews and the Neighboring Peoples of Eastern and Western Europe" (Goldin 1989), contains compelling examples of bridges between Jewish, Romanian, and Ukrainian music traditions. More recently, lectures by Americans Walter Zev Feldman (2000, 2001) and Martin Schwartz (2000) expanded on this approach, emphasizing klezmer's Greek, Turkish, and Rom connections. Intercultural connections also figure into Joel Rubin's 1998 research on Israel's *Haredi* (religious) klezmorim and Walter Zev Feldman's observations in a 1998 lecture about klezmorim in Galicia.

Klezmer history has been examined by several Israeli writers, including Joachim Stutschewsky (1959), a scion of a klezmer family who gathered together a large amount of information on the klezmer traditions of pre-state Palestine. A fellow Israeli, Isaac Rivkind (1960), expends a great deal of energy in his klezmer volume challenging Stutschewsky's methodology, and Joachim Braun (1987) contextualizes much of the older European literature on klezmer, mostly exploring the work of the descendants of klezmer families who became active in various branches of Russian concert music. In his 1998 CD titled "The Klezmer Tradition in the Land of Israel," Yaakov Mazor documents the repertoire of klezmorim that play for the *Haredi* (ultra-Orthodox and Hasidic) community.

I have chosen to take an ethnographic approach to Philadelphia's klezmer scene to highlight cross-cultural connections and bring social, cultural, and historical issues to light that mere musical analysis will tend to overlook. I also consider it important to establish a concrete relationship between a musical world and the society that spawned it. In their 1955 classic, *Hear Me Talkin' to Ya,* Nat Hentoff and Nat Shapiro bring the jazz scene vividly alive by including Earl Hines's memories of gangsters, Bunk Johnson's descriptions of "real" jam sessions, and Jelly Roll Morton's eloquent commentaries on nude dancing in New Orleans. In *Only a Miner,* Archie Green (1972) brings coal miner's ballads to life by showing how they relate to actual historical events. In *Last Night's Fun,* Ciaran Carson (1997) takes the reader deep into the world of Irish (Galway-style) *ceili* (music sessions) to meet the musicians, taste the food and liquor, feel the passage of time, and get into the spirit of Celtic folklore—presenting a convincing argument that listening to a recording is no substitute for experiencing a culture.

Evocative ethnographic writing on vernacular music can also be found in *Stomping the Blues,* Albert Murray's 1976 work on African American religious and dance music traditions. Here, dance music is given its due as a significant cultural force:

> The quality of dance music may actually be of far greater fundamental significance than that of concert music anyway. Dance, after all, not only antedates music, but is also probably the most specific source of music and most of the other art forms as well. . . . Furthermore, dance, according to impressive anthropological data, seems to have been the first means by which human consciousness objectified, symbolized, and stylized its perceptions, conceptions, and feelings. (Murray 1976: 189)

Murray includes other statements about the blues that could easily be applied both to klezmer's bittersweet mood and its significance in Jewish communal celebrations: "Hence the dance hall as temple. . . . Ballroom dances . . . are of their very nature festive occasions . . . but even the most exuberant stomp rendition is likely to contain some trace of sadness as a sobering reminder that life is at bottom, for all the very best of good times, a never-ending struggle" (17).

When music is intertwined with community life it reflects the nature of that life. When it finds its way to the concert hall, its status may become elevated, but its function in the community changes radically:

> It provides a showcase for the new and serves as a permanent gallery, so to speak, for the enduring. Moreover, as in the case of the great masterpieces of European church music, it affords opportunities for the music to be heard on its own, apart from its role as an element in a ritual, in other words as a work of art per se. . . . [The concert hall] can serve as a finger-snapping, foot-tapping annex auditorium. (Murray 1976: 183)

Murray points out that concert music is about displaying works of genius, creations of icons. In contrast, the world of the dance musician is a more conservative one, a world of folk expression drawing on habit and time-honored tradition:

> The assumption that folk expression is the unalloyed product of a direct stimulus/response interaction with natural environmental forces is fallacious. Folk expression is nothing if not conventional in the most fundamental sense of the word. Far from being spontaneous, as is so often supposed, it is formal. It is of its very nature traditional. The exact opposite of unadulterated invention, growing out of the creative ingenuity of individuals uninhibited by regulations and unencumbered by the whims of fashion, it conforms to rigorously restrictive local, regional, which is to say provincial, ground rules that have been so completely established and accepted as to require little if any enforcement as such beyond initiation and apprenticeship instruction. (Murray 1976: 203–204)

So much of traditional klezmer history is precisely what Murray describes— the learning of provincial ground rules through initiation and apprenticeship. Individuals stretch the rules according to their creative abilities, but the greatest barometer of change is approval or rejection by the community. Indeed, for the dance musician, it is the community that primarily initiates the need for innovation, not the musician.

In working on this project, I have learned that it is only through the understanding of an intact community's entire operating system that one can truly gain insight into the workings of music in culture. Ethnomusicological and cross-cultural approaches have done much to open up avenues of research into klezmer, but the fundamental relationship between the American incarnation of ethnic musics and the immigrant communities that created them still remains to be explored. This relationship, in this case between the klezmer tradition and Philadelphia's Jewish community, is precisely what this study is about.

This work is divided into two main sections. The first three chapters focus on klezmer musicians, and Chapters 4 and 5 examine wedding music traditions.

Chapter 1 considers the historical place of the musician in Jewish society, following klezmorim from their origins in medieval Europe through the 1800s. In this chapter I explore the biblical roots of the tensions between musicians and the rabbinical authorities, as entertainers established their role in providing an alternative form of enlightenment for the Jewish community. I then consider the place of music in Jewish society, examining texts that condemn music's potential for engendering moral degeneracy and presenting the restrictions that have traditionally prevented folk performers and entertainers from transcending their underclass status. This chapter also includes insights into the klezmer lifestyle, introducing the reader to both real and folkloric klezmorim. We learn about *klezmerloshn,* the Jewish musicians' secret language; hear about the coarse treatment that musicians often afforded one another and their patrons; and become acquainted with klezmer's musical transmission process through the memoirs of a nineteenth-century musician. This exploration of klezmer's European roots is essential to understanding the attitudes of and toward the American musicians I discuss later.

Chapters 2 and 3 present the history of Philadelphia's klezmer community. In Chapter 2, I trace klezmer's development from the earliest days of Eastern European immigration through its transformation in the hands of the first American-born generation, paying particular attention to the unique circumstances that made Philadelphia particularly rich as a klezmer scene. We meet transplanted old-world musicians and see how musicians from a younger generation (circa 1920) reconcile their European musical roots with their desire to become American. I also examine the standardization that occurred as Philadelphia's Jewish bandleaders consolidated their repertoire into a singular and unique local canon.

Chapter 3 picks up after World War II, when a second American generation took up a tradition that had, by then, become somewhat of a relic. I look at the competition that emerged between Jewish "society" and "traditional" bandleaders, showing how the demise of traditional musical practices reflected larger trends in post–World War II Jewish society. I also consider the various types of "revival" and "heritage" bands that emerged in Philadelphia beginning in the early 1980s.

Chapter 4 examines the klezmer's musical contribution to Philadelphia's Jewish weddings. This chapter has three sections—beginning with a review of the European Jewish wedding music repertoire, continuing with a look at a typical Philadelphia Jewish wedding circa 1905, and concluding with the actual sequence of musical events at a "standard" mid-twentieth-century Philadelphia wedding (circa 1930–1960).

Chapter 5 focuses entirely on the origins and development of Philadelphia's Russian Sher medley, a string of dance tunes that epitomizes the European roots of the traditional American Jewish wedding. I examine how the music played for the sher evolved in Philadelphia's Jewish community over the course of more than fifty years, following it through its historical journey as codified versions emerged, small instrumental groupings gave way to larger ones (and, later, to smaller regroupings), older European-style sections became interspersed with more contemporary material, meticulous transcriptions were abandoned in favor of half-remembered fragments, and a gradual decline in interest led to the dance's disappearance and the medley's obsolescence. In the process, I attempt to extract the story that the sher medley tells us about the musicians who created it and the community that reveled to it at their celebrations.

In the Epilogue, I discuss my own efforts to reenact a 1940s-style Jewish wedding on the outskirts of Philadelphia, in Cherry Hill, New Jersey, as part of Living Traditions' Klezkamp in December 2000. Enlisting the help of a local veteran caterer/dance leader and a distinguished group of Philadelphia and New

York musicians, I staged a celebration almost in real time, replete with a Grand March, phony telegrams, and a twenty-five-minute *mezinke* ceremony, proving that you can go home again, especially when you need to collect some data. And, before I knew it, this exercise took on the life of a real party, with real laughter, real tears, real romance, a fair amount of shtick, and even a little bit of community building. Who knows what might have happened if actual food and liquor had been added to the mix?

Klezmer is a body of music that is once again in circulation in many parts of the world. It provides flavor for film and theatrical scores, family parties, classroom curricula, symphonic pieces, improvisational excursions, and even religious services. But by itself, the music is now often only a symbol, a tease, a keepsake that pays a small deference to a lost world and then takes its place in a contemporary musical culture that has no use for its historical context. Perhaps, by shedding some light on that context, the role of klezmer at community celebrations, I can help foster a deeper understanding of the music as a tradition with thick layers of meaning accumulated on a long journey.

I

The Klezmer Musician

1

The Klezmer Mystique

W hile Philadelphia's Jewish wedding music, musicians, and rituals are very much a product of late nineteenth- and early twentieth-century American Jewish society, I contend that they are in just as many ways connected to the long historical continuum of musicians and entertainers who have entertained at celebrations throughout Jewish history. I am referring not only to the obvious musical connections that link generations of klezmorim together but also to the deep spiritual affinities that persist to the present day and connect them to the broader cross-cultural musician community. To put klezmorim's long-term contributions into perspective, we must examine the historical place of instrumental musicians in both Jewish and non-Jewish society.

For many generations, musicians have occupied a unique position in society, one that has both accorded them an indispensable role and burdened them with a precarious underclass status. The societal standing of Jewish folk instrumentalists has been subject not only to the nearly universal negative views of folk musicians but also to rabbinical teachings and talmudic literature on the nature and value of instrumental music. These teachings, many of which are quite restrictive and pejorative, are at the core of the tension that has always set the klezmer at a distance from other elements of Jewish society. Indeed, they all but necessitate the renegade position the klezmer has tended to inhabit.

With music occupying such a fundamentally controversial place in Jewish society, it is not surprising that even in the biblical era, musicians sometimes found themselves treated less than respectfully, as in the book of Nehemiah (7:66) where they find their way into the census only after the servants and just before the horses and donkeys (*The Writings: Kethubim* 1982: 488).[1] As the story of the klezmer unfolds, it becomes clear that the relationship between musicians and the Jewish community has always been a complex one, worthy of careful examination.

Rabbinical Restrictions

The first and most powerful set of restrictions on klezmorim came from decrees by rabbinical authorities. Those cited most often are regulations put into practice as a consequence of the destruction of the Second Jewish Temple by the Romans in 70 C.E. (A.D.). These statutes ostensibly banished instrumental music and joyous singing from religious observance as a sign of mourning. The biblical passage usually quoted as the source of the prohibition is found in Lamentations 5:14 (*The Lamentations of Jeremiah*): "The elders have ceased from the gate, the young men from their music." The most extreme interpretation of this passage, still adhered to by some ultra-Orthodox movements, forbids instrumental music in any form at any time. Amnon Shiloah cites various quotes often used to reinforce such an interpretation, including passages by Rabbi Moses ben Maimon (Maimonides; 1135–1204), excerpts from the talmudic book of Sotah, and the pronouncements of Rabbi Joseph Han-Nordlingen (died 1637), including this one: "And above all, musical instruments are forbidden at feasts; they are prohibited even if there is no feast" (Shiloah 1992: 74).

Shiloah adds that, among the ultra-Orthodox, strict adherence to laws relating to the destruction of the Temple requires one to mourn in a way that is real and perpetual, with the circumstances of mourning apparent even on occasions normally calling for joy, such as a bridal celebration. At all times one is expected to share in Israel's sorrow and never forget that the divine presence has been exiled from the land; joy and music are to be relegated to the time of redemption. Proponents of the banning of music often quote passages from Sotah, which call for "desolation in the house" and proclaim that "the ear that hears song will be cut off" (Shiloah 1992: 75).

In addition to passages that cite mourning for the Temple as the reason for a ban on instrumental music ban, a much larger body of Jewish religious literature sees music as an intrinsically controversial pursuit. According to this commonplace Orthodox rabbinical perspective, music by itself (i.e., without a religious connection) can be quite dangerous and, by definition, be associated with corruption and moral degeneracy. The basis for this belief is found in the biblical account of music's origin. In midrash (often-quoted narrative elaborations of biblical stories), Jubal, the inventor not only of music but also of singing and all manner of instruments, is thought to be a son of Cain, the originator of many forms of corruption including, of course, murder. Rabbi Eliezer (circa 45–117 C.E.) writes of how Na'ama, a daughter of Cain, seduced the pure offspring of the sons of Seth with song, dance, instrumental music, and intoxicating drink. The resulting debauchery is later cited as the impetus for a deluge that was meant to destroy their entire generation (Shiloah 1992: 79).

The writings of Maimonides, an extraordinarily influential thinker who lived and worked as a physician in Spain during one of the golden periods of Jewish medieval philosophy, are the source of many restrictions pertaining to music. In answering a question posed by Jews in Aleppo who sought permission to listen to regional Arabic music (singing accompanied by a reed pipe), Maimonides reiterates the traditional point of view that all music meant for amusement is strictly forbidden. He then gives a six-point summary of prohibitions on music, listed in ascending order of severity:

1. Listening to a song with a secular text, whether it be in Hebrew or Arabic
2. Listening to a song accompanied by an instrument
3. Listening to a song whose content includes obscene language
4. Listening to a stringed instrument
5. Listening to passages played on such instruments while drinking wine[2]
6. Listening to the singing and playing of a woman (Shiloah 1992: 74)

These restrictions have nothing to do with the destruction of the Temple and have no bearing on religious music. Their purpose is to legislate a total ban on secular musical expression. It is with such sources in mind that rabbinical authorities have done their best to restrict and regulate the place of celebratory music in Jewish society over the years.[3]

The notion that instrumental music is intrinsically "un-Jewish" continues to prevail in some Orthodox circles, and the talmudically proscribed hierarchy privileging male vocal music with sacred text over any other music and limiting instrumental music to the accompaniment of such texts has had a profound impact on the study of Jewish music over the years (Idelsohn 1929: 18). Indeed, by virtue of their myriad restrictions, the Orthodox rabbinate has, in effect, confined instrumental musicians to the secular world, inadvertently according them an apostate position as emissaries to an alternative path to spiritual elevation.

The Kabbalistic and Hasidic Perspective

In later years, kabbalistic[4] and Hasidic[5] masters dismissed various restrictive pronouncements concerning musical abstinence, especially those connected with the "perpetual state of mourning." In their view, music was a necessary outgrowth of human beings' intrinsic need for joy and was indeed permissible as long as it was played with the proper intention (a view actually consonant with that of Maimonides, whose restrictions only covered secular musical expression). Indeed, the very first biblical mention of *kle zemer* (lit. "vessels of song") in 2 Kings 3:15 has been interpreted as a sign that musicians played an important role and had significant responsibilities within the Israelite community during the biblical and post-Temple eras: "Now then, get me a musician. As the musician played, the hand of the Lord was upon him" (2 Kings 3:15) (*The Prophets: Nevi'im* 1978: 289).

Some Hasidim have interpreted this passage to mean that the player and the instrument should be considered as one (indeed the Hebrew phrase *kle zemer* seems to refer to both the instrument and the player), that every thought of the musician should concern only the music he is playing, and that he should make his music so that "the hand of the Lord" will lay upon the people (Berlin 2000, pers. comm.). From this perspective, music is to be used only as a means to bring heavenly inspiration to the Jewish nation. While such a viewpoint may be seen as a noble one and is compatible with the lifestyles of present-day *Haredi* (religious) klezmorim in Israel and elsewhere, it hardly reflects the worldview or aesthetic orientation of most Jewish instrumentalists, who tend to keep their distance from organized religion.[6]

With knowledge of this biblical literature in mind, rabbis nonetheless sought to find justification for the inclusion of secular (or, at least, popular co-territorial) instrumental music in various types of celebrations. There is ample evidence of such music being played as part of the celebration of the festival of Purim and at weddings as early as the beginning of the Common Era.

Klezmorim and Badkhonim

The *kle zemer* of the post-Temple era is barely mentioned in Jewish literature until he emerges as a medieval minstrel (now known by the Yiddish term "klezmer" or the German term *Spielmann)* in the 1400s. Written records of that time tell of guilds of Jewish musicians in Frankfurt that provided music for weekly dances. Ghetto musicians were also employed at three- or seven-day Jewish wedding celebrations and at Christian banquets as well. We know that these musical groups consisted of both men and women and that, although they played most types of instruments available where they lived, they preferred those of the string family (Feldman 2001). The klezmer's early fellow traveler, the *leyts* (jester), can be traced back to the thirteenth century, while the *badkhn* (a moralizing folk poet) emerged in Poland in the 1500s (Lifshutz 1952: 44).

While we have no way of knowing precisely how the music of early klezmorim sounded or what repertoire they played (aside from certain general dance genres), the distinctive style of Jewish instrumental performance was noted relatively early on. Even in the medieval Frankfort *tanzhauf* (dance court), Jewish musicians were eventually segregated to "Jewish *Tanzhusen*" so that non-Jewish musicians would not pick up Jewish "nuances." In an attempt to silence the klezmorim of Prague, a petition written by Christian musicians noted, "The Jewish musicians corrupt and confuse the music, because they do not follow either tempo or time signature, thus mockingly depriving the noble and charming music of its esteemed quality" (Sendrey 1970: 353).[7]

As the Jewish population spread through Central and Eastern Europe, klezmorim became fixtures in virtually every community. By the middle to late

1500s there were large Jewish communities in Constantinople (Istanbul), Prague, Lemberg (Lwow), Lublin, Krakow, and Budapest (Sendrey 1970: 356) and in many parts of Romania, Galicia, and the Ukraine.[8] Because Jews were not allowed to attend conservatories in any part of Europe until the mid-1800s, those with musical talent who wished to retain their religious and ethnic identity had little choice but to embrace the folk musician status that the klezmer profession implied.

References from the earliest period of documentation (the 1400s) tell us that klezmorim came from musical families that tended to interconnect through marriage and thereby produce new generations of Jewish musicians. In most locales, their position in both Jewish and general society was precarious, in that they were subject to heavy taxation, but had limited access to public performance by the secular authorities and, as noted earlier, were victims of the general condescension of the rabbinical leadership.

Still, their function was considered essential. In the fourteenth century, the *Maharal* (Jewish community leader) of Mainz, a major rabbinical figure of the time, was faced with the prospect of a wedding taking place in his principality during a period of mourning that had been declared in one of his districts. To ensure the participation of klezmorim, he moved the celebration to another district, proclaiming the function of music at a Jewish wedding to be so essential that, if the wedding were to take place on the Jewish Sabbath, he would bring in gentile musicians to entertain (Strom 2002: 7).

In the early days of klezmorim and badkhonim, the wrath of the religious establishment fell most heavily on the latter, whose mock religious commentary (known as *badkhones*) ranged from profoundly scholarly to heavily sardonic. This type of Jewish folk poet was most likely modeled after the German *marshalik* (with some resemblance to the *minnesinger,* but without the Christian connotations) and was sometimes referred to by the German term. The role of the badkhn was also closely related to that of the Russian *tysiatskii* (master of ceremonies), but in the Jewish incarnation, it always included mock religious duties that were entirely foreign to non-Jewish wedding entertainers. Comedic Jewish folk poets were also referred to as *leytsim* or *letsonim* (jesters), a term sometimes used as a substitute label for klezmorim or any other kind of Jewish entertainer.

For as long as they have existed (and one can assume they predate the written references), klezmorim and badkhonim have symbolized an alternative form of expression within Jewish society, and their presence at pivotal community celebrations, such as weddings, has always ensured them a sizable audience. In "Merrymakers and Jesters among Jews," Lifschutz (1952: 43) explains how the common people welcomed their performances as a foil to the rigorous moralistic scrutiny of the religious leadership:

> All the complaints by the rabbis and the criticism of communal leaders that weddings were being transformed from sacred events to secular gatherings, in which jest, humor, satire and dance were the most important

components, were to no avail. The masses of people, yearning for amusement and frequently having to seek it outside the ghetto, seized upon a wedding as a legitimate opportunity for such amusement. Even the more prominent citizens also enjoyed a jest and a quip no less than the more humble Jew. The wedding celebration provided the Jew with practically the only opportunity for such recreation.

The spirit of the post-ceremony wedding celebration was in many ways comparable to the mood of the Purim holiday festivities,[9] in which a "carnivalesque" spirit prevailed.[10] Such a tone contrasted greatly with the somber mood of the pre-ceremony and the ceremony itself, which contained ritual elements strikingly similar to those of the Day of Atonement. These rituals included a day of fasting for the bride and groom and the recitation of prayers for the dead at the family's cemetery plot.

Ironically, the details of the carrying-on that took place at early wedding celebrations are primarily chronicled in rabbinical tomes that malign such festivities. Such moralistic guides as the *Seyfer Midos* (Book of *Midos* [positive character traits]) and the *Lev Tov* (Good Heart) deride marshaliks for engaging in lascivious talk, impudent speech, and levity in the place of more modest expression. More pious scholars even offered alternative wedding verses to counteract the rowdy poetry of badkhonim, such as the song mentioned in this passage by seventeenth-century talmudist Elhanan Hirshahn quoted in Lifschutz (1952: 52):

> There is cheering, shouting and singing, clapping of hands, stamping of feet and jumping on the tables. Women and girls help out with shrieking like harlots. In order to banish the impudent songs, I composed this song for weddings and circumcision rites.

The badkhn or marshalik produced risqué rhymes at the *khusn's tish*, the male gathering held at the groom's table before the wedding; introspective laments at the *kale's bazetsn* and *badekn*, the bride's seating and veiling; and tactless appraisals of gifts at the *droshe geshenk*, a takeoff on the rabbinical *droshe*, in which a biblical text is analyzed and interpreted. In this case, the droshe geshenk refers to a ceremony during which the gifts are enumerated and evaluated. At times badkhonim would juggle, impersonate women in labor, mimic ecstatic Hasidim, dress up as circus bears, or feign the guise of Cossacks (Sapoznik 1999: 16, 17). It is hardly surprising that such antics, along with their wry brand of biblical analysis, routinely got the badkhonim into trouble with religious authorities.

In addition, the Jewish instrumentalists of the Middle Ages had to contend with another type of stigma: their societal disreputability. All European folk musicians of that era was denied many legal rights, including membership in trade guilds and land ownership (prior to 1648). Their status was not helped by the fact that their work was perceived as satisfying the baser needs of the upper class; they were routinely suspected of paganism, thievery, and sorcery (Krickberg 1983: 121). In some areas (especially parts of Germany) klezmorim had to deal with three sets of restrictions: those imposed on all musicians, those imposed by the secular authorities on Jewish musicians, and those imposed on Jewish musicians by the Jews themselves. It is not surprising that they had trouble making a decent living. Indeed, some converted to Christianity, so that they might find opportunities in classical or church music or employment as instrument builders.

Lives of the Klezmorim

Outside of demographic data, there exists little documentation of the lives of klezmorim before the nineteenth century. By this time, the klezmer repertoire was primarily a mixture of Romanian, Greek, Moldavian, Ukrainian, Gypsy, and Jewish (especially Hasidic) elements. Many of the most popular Jewish dance steps, especially those popular among Jews living in Galicia, Bessarabia (Moldova), and the southern Ukraine, were also borrowed from various co-territorialists.

Part of an early klezmer memoir is found in Beregovski 2001, which includes quotations from an autobiography written in 1830 by a semi-professional musician named Bogrov. Here we find a definitive account of the klezmer transmission process, which bears out the commonly held belief that the repertoire was learned by rote:

> I took lessons diligently and would practice for several hours at a time. The master of the black fiddle (Reb Leivick) had no method of instruction. . . . written music was Greek to the maestro and his associates; they taught me by demonstration, straight from the fingers. Nonetheless, I made quick progress, and Reb Leivik took pride in me as living testimony to the efficacy of his method.[11] (Beregovski 2001: 30)

The most celebrated virtuoso klezmer of all time was probably Joseph Michael Gusikov (1809–1837), who was born in Shklov, Mogilev *gubernia* (province), Belarus, to a klezmer family that had produced several generations of excellent flutists. Forced to abandon the flute at an early age because of illness, young Joseph Michael took up the "straw fiddle," a kind of folk xylophone with bars arranged in a *tsimbl*-like (Romanian hammered dulcimer) tuning pattern. Gusikov's Orthodox garb helped him cultivate an "exotic" image, although the actual extent of his observance is still hotly debated.[12] He concertized extensively during his brief lifetime, earning the praise of many of Europe's finest musicians, including Felix Mendelssohn, who called him a "true genius" (Beregovski 2001: 23), and the disdain of others, such as Felix's sister Fanny Mendelssohn, who called him a "fox" (Sapoznik 1999: 4).

Other much-heralded nineteenth-century klezmorim were violinists Yossele Drucker (1822–1879), better known as "Stempenyu" and made famous by a semi-biographical Sholem Aleichem novel, and Aron-Moyshe Kholodenko (1828–1902), also known as "Pedotser," several of whose elaborate compositions have survived in manuscript.[13] The universal success of these musicians underscored the ability of nineteenth-century klezmorim to transcend the narrow limits of their prescribed role within Jewish society and cross over to the concert stage, where their flamboyance was considered an undisputed asset.

Also courtesy of Beregovski, we do have one relatively detailed account of the career of a nineteenth-century klezmer. Avram Yehoshua Makonovetskii (a respondent to Beregovski's early twentieth-century klezmer survey) was born in Khabno (Kiev gubernia) in 1872. His father worked as a violinist, watchmaker, barber, and glazier, and Avram began playing tambourine in his father's band at age eight, earning forty kopeks (a Polish monetary unit) per wedding. With the aid of his father's tutelage, he was soon able to function as second violinist, which earned him a raise to sixty kopeks.[14] However, he was treated poorly by his father and left for Radomysl, where there was a musically better klezmer band whose leader came from a well-known klezmer family. Returning to Khabno in 1893, he put together a band that included ten instrumentalists (violins, trumpets, flute, clarinet, trombone, cello, and drums).

"In the eyes of the small-town public," Makonovetskii writes, "the musician's trade was exceedingly low-class. Musicians were accorded all kinds of disdainful nicknames."[15] Despite such aspersions, he retained a high opinion of his chosen (and sole) profession. His *kapelye* (band) served the towns within a forty- or fifty-mile radius, playing their klezmer repertoire for Jews and non-Jews alike, but only ballroom dances for the wealthier citizens.

The Klezmer in Literature

While Makonovetskii's descriptions tell us a great deal about the nuts and bolts of the klezmer profession, they reveal very little about the klezmer's lifestyle and character. For this we need to turn to literary sources. Many Yiddish writers took note of klezmorim, remarking on the transcendent power of musicians. This passage from a nineteenth-century memoir introduces us to a klezmer who lived near Uman in the southern Ukraine:

(Khayim Klezmer) was a real artist, with big, dreamy eyes, a pale, gaunt face, and fingers long, thin, white and sensitive. He knew almost nothing of the real world: any child could take advantage of him . . . but when he placed his cheek against the fiddle and first drew the bow across the strings, he would open up a truly new world for you. You felt that a captive soul, hidden in his fiddle, was trying to break free—it wailed, wept, and begged. . . . Men with long beards and hardened faces became like small children when they heard Khayim the klezmer. One wanted to cuddle up to someone, to be babied like a child by its mother, to lament one's bitter fate. (Moissye Olgin, cited in Beregovski 2001: 22–23)

In a passage from *Stempenyu* (the novel about Yossele Drucker, mentioned earlier), Sholom Rabinovitsh, much better known by his pen name Sholem Aleichem, attributes to the klezmer a kind of power over people's emotions and feelings that one would think might be reserved for a religious leader:

> The public sits very respectfully, and the klezmer plays a sad piece. . . . the fiddle cries, dissolves in the lower strings, and the other fellows support him very sadly. A bit of melancholy falls on the audience and everyone gets pensive. Everyone is lost in thought and puts his nose down and, rubbing his fingers on the plate or kneading a crumb of the fresh bread, steeps himself in his thoughts, his sad thoughts, since probably everyone has his worries, and a Jew doesn't need to borrow trouble. (Rabinovitsh, cited in Slobin 1982: 17)

In another passage, the great storyteller underscores the marginal nature of wedding musicians in relation to the more respectable elements in Jewish society:

> The young man . . . is a klezmer. A really fine young man. . . . May God send him his intended, which he deserves. . . . And may the almighty choose something else for her daughter whence her husband, may he rest in peace, didn't play the fiddle, nor did his father, nor his father's father. (Rabinovitsh 1979: 25)

If Sholem Aleichem's klezmorim are romantic outcasts who inhabit a secret, mysterious world, Isaac Bashevis Singer's wedding musicians are portrayed as actual threats to the status quo. In his story, "The Dead Fiddler," he tells of a woman possessed by the soul of a fiddler named Getsl, a dead klezmer who is the epitome of licentiousness, drunkenness, and blasphemy. In the following conversation between a pious father and a klezmer dybbuk (disembodied spirit), Singer beautifully encapsulates the age-old gulf between the klezmer's worldview and the sanitized facade of mainstream Jewish society:

> "Why did you choose to enter my daughter?" [Reb Sheftel] asked in desperation.
> "Why not? She's a good-looking girl. I hate the ugly ones—always have, always will." With that, the dybbuk began to shout ribaldries and obscenities, both in ordinary Yiddish and in musician's slang. . . . "Will you bring me a glass of liquor or won't you?"
> "And what if we don't?"
> "If you don't, I'll lay you all wide open, you pious hypocrites. And the secrets of your wives—may they burn up with hives."

"... Evil spirit, I command you to leave the body of my innocent daughter ..."

"In another minute you'll have me scared! You think you're so strong because your beard's long?"

"Impudent wretch, betrayer of Israel!"

"Better an open rake than a sanctimonious fake." (Singer 1982: 222)

Later in the story, a second dybbuk enters the young woman's body; eventually, the two dybbuks are persuaded to get married. Here, Singer's (1982: 230) fictional account of their wedding brings alive the world of the European klezmer:

Getsl proved that evening that he was not only an expert musician but could also serve as rabbi, cantor, and wedding jester. First he played a sad tune and recited "God Is Full of Mercy" for the bride and groom. Then he played a merry tune, accompanying it with appropriate jests. He admonished the bride to be a faithful wife, to dress and adorn herself, and to take good care of her household. He warned the couple to be mindful of the day of death. . . . Although it was a mock wedding many a tear fell from the women's eyes.

Singer's passages beautifully illustrate the klezmer's ability to embrace ritual while eschewing piety. Unfortunately, such a brash public persona placed wedding entertainers at the fringe of image-conscious Jewish society, in a position comparable to that of Gypsies in the greater European world. Treated as superhuman and subhuman at the same time, they were considered welcome only when needed for their talents and otherwise thought to be "outside the pale of regular community life" (Slobin 1982: 16). They were seen as itinerants, sleeping virtually anywhere but home, gambling and drinking at every opportunity, and doing their best to beat the system in every way. Their strongly male-dominated culture was keenly focused on preserving their turf and maximizing their earnings. In a world where book knowledge and money were badges of success, they had little to show for all of their efforts; often their status was compared with that of beggars.[16]

Many of these stereotypes and folkloric images contrasted sharply with what we now know about some actual klezmorim, who had permanent home bases, relatively normal family lives, a variety of musical skills, and moderately lucrative day jobs.[17] Still, we must keep in mind that such stereotypes always contain a grain of truth. While the klezmer's business acumen and mobility were roughly comparable to those of Jews in other professions, it is clear that many of his co-religionists considered him intrinsically irresponsible, sexually active, and violent.

Notwithstanding the behavior of any particular family or musician, the klezmer's life was a life apart. Much of his private world found its verbal expression in *klezmerloshn*, the secret klezmer argot that included key terms needed to conduct business in the profession. Some klezmerloshn terms were shared with thieves' slang (*bash* for "money," *matren* for "look," *drizhblen* for "sleep with"), while others pertained only to music (*shoyfer* for "trumpet," *tshekal* for "drum"). Other expressions were quite colorful, with extra layers of meaning: *kapure* (sin offering) for "married woman," *yold* (chump) for "employer," *fardreyen zikh* (get twisted) for "get married" (Rothstein 2002: 28–29). Moreover, klezmorim were often known only by nicknames, usually entwined with the name of the instrument they played, or by colorful stage names.

Hiring a klezmer band was not always a straightforward process. To secure the services of a kapelye, the father of the bride negotiated with the klezmer in charge, who then negotiated with the head of the local guild, if guilds were in place, or with the local klezmorim if the group was not from the immediate area and no guild existed. In many cases the musicians would pay a sum or give up an item of collateral to secure the engagement. In a world where musicians were deeply mistrusted this practice was seen as the only way to ensure that the band would show up and play.[18] The size and instrumentation of the ensemble varied, depending on local rules concerning noise, but in most areas ensembles consisted of four to six musicians (usually mostly string players) until the late 1800s when such restrictions were relaxed.

Folkloric images play themselves out in twentieth-century klezmer accounts. Although klezmorim and badkhonim coexisted as wedding entertainers, we know that their relationship was sometimes far from cordial. The renowned nineteenth-century badkhn, Eliakhum Zunser, spoke of rough treatment by klezmorim in his memoir:

> In the beginning I earned very little at my new business. I was only called to poor weddings and was poorly paid, and second I had to have music to accompany my recitation of my songs and the musicians would take all my earnings from my pocket. If they could not do this at the wedding itself, they would fall upon me in the street, when I was going home from the wedding, push me against the wall, and rob me of my money. (Zunser, quoted in Lifshutz 1952: 75)

Musicians were also coarse with one another, especially when a "foreign" kapelye invaded another band's home turf. Records of fistfights between competing groups of musicians date back many centuries. As noted earlier, the klezmer caste was, in general, not the most genteel element of Jewish society. The character of a typical klezmer-style interaction is reflected in this passage from an interview with Ben Bazyler, a twentieth-century klezmer from a small town near Warsaw:

> In those days, no one was shy. Once *feter* [uncle] Nusn had to tell the bass player off, and he made him feel like dirt. Why? "Nobody likes a loser; everybody likes a winner." When he sensed a soft spot he went for it. Do you understand? Could you say that they were *proste mentshn* [coarse people]? (Alpert 1990: 50)

Sexual virility is another important staple of klezmer lore that entered musicians' memoirs again and again. The linkage of Jewish musicians with both sexual attraction and promiscuity remained significant and was borne out in interviews with many contemporary European and American klezmorim. Here Ben Bazyler elucidates on a fantasy of this sort:

> The girl with the kerosene? How did she put it? "The musicians are playing so well that I could go to bed with them." Did you understand how she said it? This is very important. Think about it: she was so excited, that's what came out of her. . . . don't forget, we're not talking about a girl of today. . . . She slept in the same bed as her mother. And she still said it. (Alpert 1990: 50)

As noted in the Introduction, such references to sex were hardly the exclusive domain of Jewish musicians and were widespread in most musicians' lore.

The European Klezmer Repertoire

As mentioned earlier, the culture that produced the music for Jewish celebrations was a rich polyglot. In his analysis of the repertoire of Eastern European klezmorim, Walter Zev Feldman (2002) distinguishes between "Jewish," transitional, and co-territorial dance genres.

"Jewish" dance genres, which sometimes had their root in ritualized ceremony, tended to be remarkably uniform over a wide geographical area, spanning eastern Ukraine, Belarus, Lithuania, eastern Poland, Moldova, Austrian Bukovina, Galicia, and Romania. The Jewish repertoire (which Feldman calls "core") included the *freylekhs* (a lively Jewish dance in duple meter, also known as *hopke, dreydl, and rikudl*); *skochne* and *sher* (two other lively duple-metered dances with more set choreography than the freylekhs); and *khusidl* (a dance that parodied the ecstatic motions of Hasidim during prayer). While these dances differed choreographically, much of their musical material seemed to have been interchangeable (Feldman 2002: 92–93). Ritual dances that were part of the "core" included the *broyges tants* (dance of anger and reconciliation); *mezinke tants* (also called the krinsl [crown], a dance in honor of the bride's mother played at the youngest daughter's wedding); and the *mitzve* (commandment) *tants* and kosher (dietary laws*) tants*, dances celebrating a commitment to traditional observance on the part of the bride and groom. The *dobridzen* (good morning tune) and *dobrinotsh* (good night tune) were also usually melodies of Jewish origin, as were *mazel-tovs* (congratulatory tunes) and processionals. Other "core" tunes corresponded to Jewish holiday observances and even included funeral dirges.

The "transitional" (or what Feldman calls "Orientalized") repertoire included dances such as the *volekhl* (slow Wallachian dance in 3/8 meter), hora (Romanian circle dance in 3/8 meter), *sirba, ange* (honga), and *bulgarish* or *bulgar* (all lively Romanian dances in duple meter). Nondance genres, such as the *doyne* (Romanian shepherd's lament) and *kale bazetsn* (lament for seating the bride) also fell into this category. Although many of these dance tunes were clearly Greco-Moldavian, Ukrainian, Gypsy, or Crimean Tatar in origin, Feldman makes a point of distinguishing them from co-territorial repertoire because of their hybrid nature and because they were popular in areas far from their geographical points of origin. They were often played in medleys along with core repertoire or were composed by klezmorim "in the style" of the ethnic groups from which they originated. It is likely that much of this transitional repertoire came into the Jewish consciousness in the late 1800s.

Nineteenth-century (and earlier) klezmorim also incorporated a large amount of co-territorial material into their repertoire. The type of material and the amount incorporated varied from region to region, so that Polish and Czech klezmorim had a wide repertoire of *mazurs* and *mazurkes*, Ruthenians played *kolomeykes*, Hungarians danced the *vengurke* and the *czardas*, and Ukrainians played the *kozachok* and *kamarinska*. In addition, klezmorim performed a wide variety of Western and Central European dance tunes, including the waltz, polka, quadrille, *pas d'espan,* and gavotte. These "cosmopolitan" genres, played for Jews and non-Jews alike, are popular wedding staples to this day.

The Culture of the Odessa Region

In many areas of Eastern Europe, Jewish culture was brought together with neighboring influences. Walter Zev Feldman's work focuses on the culture of the borderlands of Austria, Hungary, and the Czech Republic, which profoundly influenced the musical world of Galician klezmorim. Since this study focuses on klezmer music that came primarily from southern Ukraine and Moldova (although it also has a profound Byelorussian component), it is more relevant to look at the culture of the Odessa region, in which Jewish culture and the klezmer repertoire were transformed by Greek and Turkish influences in the late 1800s. In that cosmopolitan Black Sea port, one might hear the same melody with lyrics in any of a dozen common languages.

Odessa was a modern city, founded in 1799, and its culture provided a rowdy, nonreligious alternative paradigm for nineteenth-century Jews. Its mixture of enterprise, license, and violence combined to create an environment free from the restraints of the past (Zipperstein 1985: 1). It is also worth noting that the Jews joined and helped create the Odessa culture precisely when the *haskalah* (enlightenment) movement was at its peak, providing them with role models that were the extreme antithesis of the German intellectuality that held forth elsewhere.

The acculturation, modernization, and secularization that took place in Odessa soon became a catalyst for the general breakdown of rabbinical Judaism, a breakdown that was centered in the Ukraine and Moldova. By the late 1880s, Minsk, Warsaw, Kovno, Brest-litovsk, Kiev, Grodno, Bialystok, Rovno, Kishinev, and Odessa were joined by rail (Zipperstein 1985: 16), and the culture of the port city and other cosmopolitan metropolises blazed an indelible path into Eastern European Jewish consciousness at the precise point when the greatest immigration to America was poised to begin.

Another factor that transformed the klezmer world in the late nineteenth century was the entry of large numbers of klezmorim into Russian military bands. In those bands they learned secondary instruments, honed their music-reading skills, and picked up new repertoire. They also made contacts that lasted throughout their professional careers.

Many klezmorim migrated to the United States during the period of greatest Eastern European Jewish immigration, between 1880 and 1924, although there were traces of their music in the Americas before that time. Once in the new world they quickly formed associations and unions,[19] and some adapted to American ways of doing business. America's immigrant neighborhoods provided new springboards for cultural mergers that made Eastern Europe seem dull by comparison. In those communities there was a chaotic din of new sounds and new opportunities. Yet many klezmorim kept their European ties by living in tight-knit immigrant enclaves and joining *landsmanshaftn*, organizations of immigrants from specific towns. The tendency of Americans to form such associations was not uniquely Jewish, having been noted by de Tocqueville as early as 1831:

> Americans of all ages, all conditions and all dispositions constantly form associations. They have not only commercial and manufacturing companies, in which all take part, but associations of a thousand other kinds, religious, moral, serious, futile, general or restricted, enormous or diminutive . . . for every purpose, from entertainment to temperance. (De Tocqueville, cited in Soyer 1997: 29)

While European klezmer orchestras were usually known by the names of their towns of origin, in the United States bands became known only by their leaders' names. Most of America's early klezmer orchestra leaders were violinists, many of whom doubled on trumpet, thanks to their forced tenure in the Russian military. Some brought over typical European klezmer instruments such as the tsimbl, straw fiddle (folk xylophone), harmonica (small accordion), bohemian flute, or rotary-valve cornet. By the 1920s, Jewish dance music instrumentation had fallen more in line with typical American vaudeville or concert bands of the time. The brass-laden sounds of these ensembles reflected the orientation of the popular bandleaders, several of whom also found work as theater orchestra directors or as associate conductors for such mainstream American figures as John Phillip Sousa and Arthur Pryor.

The period of immigration coincided with the beginning of the era of recorded music. Anonymous traditional dance tunes were soon given titles and marketed as "ethnic music."[20] While the Jewish dances reproduced on 78 RPM recordings give us precious little insight into the personalities, lives, and interactions of their creators,[21] they do provide us with an outline of essential klezmer repertoire from the early immigrant era. Most of the popular European genres were captured on early recordings, although others seemed to have been abandoned on the trip over. Klezmorim brought regional tunes to their adopted American communities, and soon every American city had its own instantly recognizable local Jewish repertoire.

The clarinet became the predominant instrument in the American bands, and several New York–based clarinetists became American klezmer icons. A scion of a renowned Hasidic klezmer dynasty from Austrian Galicia, Naftule Brandwein (1889–1963) was acclaimed for his expressive playing and showed mastery of a tremendous variety of rhythmic and coloristic subtleties. Teplek-born (southern Ukraine) Dave Tarras (1897–1991) earned a reputation as the undisputed technical wizard of the music, with quick trills and finger gymnastics that rivaled any classical soloist.[22] His career lasted well into the 1980s, and his later recordings show his emotional side to great effect. Shloimke Beckerman (1889–1974) played in a heavily ornamented and rhythmically propulsive style. Max Epstein (1913–2000) synthesized the approaches of Brandwein and Tarras, while also drawing on the inspiration of his early Bessarabian (Moldavian) mentors. He and his brothers are credited with introducing contemporary harmonic ideas to the music.

Accomplished performers also recorded on other instruments. Accordionist Misha Tziganoff (dates unknown) played virtually every Eastern European musical style with impeccable authenticity, and tsimblist Joseph Moscovitz (1879–1954) held forth at his own Romanian restaurant in New York, performing everything from doynes (unmetered Romanian laments) to ragtime. The career of percussionist Jacob ("Jakey") Hoffman (1895–1972) is discussed in Chapter 2.

Few of the American performers of this era actually called themselves klezmorim, and the term is found nowhere in the title of any Jewish instrumental recording of the time. While the musicians were aware of their continuity in a long line of wedding entertainers (and, in some cases, their direct connection to distinguished klezmer families), they tended to think of a klezmer as a vestige of old Europe. They used the term only as a derogatory way to refer to those whom they felt could not adapt to the demands of the contemporary American music scene (an ironic turn of events, since many of these same musicians had been considered models of versatility while in Europe). Indeed, such adaptation went both ways, and non-Jewish musicians became very much in demand for work in Jewish orchestras.

The klezmer took his place at the table in his new American home. Here there were a variety of transported immigrant musics alongside vibrant African American traditions, all feeding into an emerging American culture with seemingly limitless boundaries. In the following chapters we see how the klezmer evolved in a new land that offered new opportunities, new challenges, and new temptations.

2

Klezmer Musicians in Jewish Philadelphia, 1900–1945

My survey of Philadelphia's klezmer tradition begins at the turn of the twentieth century. This was an era when, to paraphrase folklorist Y. L. Cahan, Jewish folklore could still be "scooped up in handfuls" (Joselit 1994: 3). It was a period of diversity, a time to celebrate a vibrant European culture, and an era of change, full of the new and strange relationships that emerge by necessity when an uprooted community finds itself in a new land. It was also an epoch when quite a few European klezmer families became well established in Philadelphia and began to disseminate a body of repertoire that became the basis of Philadelphia's klezmer music tradition.

When Eastern European Jewish immigrants began to arrive in Philadelphia in the late 1800s, they found themselves face to face with a well-established and secure German and Sephardic (tracing their roots to Spain) Jewish community that had flourished in the city since pre-Revolutionary times. However, compared to other North American cities, Philadelphia was unusually hospitable to its Jewish immigrants;[1] consequently, by the end of World War I, Jews constituted the city's largest immigrant group (Tabak 1990: 9). In the early years of the twentieth century, Philadelphia boasted the third largest Jewish community in the United States, behind only New York and Chicago.

While scant information is available concerning Philadelphia's earliest klezmorim, we do know that many of these musicians began to arrive around 1881 as part of the first large wave of Eastern European Jewish refugees.[2] News of economic opportunities, combined with a deterioration of conditions for Jews in czarist Russia (due to an acceleration of anti-Semitic attacks in the Ukraine beginning in 1881), prompted a steady flow of Jewish immigrants into American cities until 1924, when the U.S. government began to impose strict quotas. Most of Philadelphia's earliest arrivals settled in the North Philadelphia neighborhood of Port Richmond, which quickly earned the nicknames of "Jerusalem" among Jews and "Jewtown" among non-Jews (Tabak 1990: 30). Soon, South Philadelphia took over as the city's principal Jewish neighborhood. By 1920, the city was home to 240,000 Jews.

In surveying the Jewish wedding music scene in Philadelphia, it is important to consider the European points of origin of Philadelphia's Jewish musicians and its Jewish community at large. The Jewish population included a large concentration of Jews from southern Ukraine and Moldova, long considered important heartlands of klezmer music, which makes the city an ideal subject for a regional klezmer study. More than 60 percent of twentieth-century Philadelphia's Jews traced their origins to Ukraine; of these Jews, a large majority came from areas near Kiev (Tabak 1990: 22). This fact alone gave Philadelphia's Jewish wedding music tradition a considerable amount of uniformity even in its early years, especially when compared to more diverse enclaves such as New York and Chicago.

These circumstances may also partially account for the longevity of older "ethnic" celebratory customs, including Eastern European dance and music traditions, in the Philadelphia Jewish community. Studies of religious customs among Jewish immigrants from various regions of Eastern Europe show that Ukrainian Jews of the immigrant generation were more inclined than Jews from elsewhere toward an ethnic, rather than formally religious, approach to life (Tabak 1990: 23). Many of the Jewish families who came to Philadelphia were worldly Jews from lapsed Hasidic backgrounds.[3] When it came time for them to affiliate with formal Jewish institutions, most ended up as Conservative rather than Orthodox Jews.

For many Philadelphia Jews, the term "Jewish" had very little to do with the idea of religion. It was not unusual for American Jews to be highly selective in their approach to ritual behavior and cultural identity, and those coming from the Ukraine and Moldova were even more selective than Jews from other backgrounds. In the 1920s and 1930s, newly settled Jewish immigrants and their offspring took every opportunity to "ignore, retain, modify, adapt, invent, reappropriate, and reconstruct tradition" (Joselit 1994: 4). It should not be surprising therefore that this was also a time when the klezmer tradition in each immigrant community took on an American context that could not have been foreseen in Europe.

Those who came to Philadelphia in the first wave of immigration did their best to continue the social affiliations they had brought with them from Europe. Immigrants maintained their European links through their membership in landsmanshaftn, synagogues, and burial societies. In many cases they also maintained allegiances to musicians who came from their towns or regions. A town's musical repertoire (and musical business) was often passed down within a family. Clarinetist Morris Hoffman, a second-generation klezmer, recalls his early initiation into music:

My father came from Kriovozer, a *shtetl* [town] in the Ukraine [approx-
imately sixty miles south of Uman].[4] He taught all six of his children to
play, and when anyone from Kriovozer had an affair, there was usually
a Hoffman in the band. [Tubist Morris] Schnitzer and violinist Itzy
Krepke were also from Kriovozer, so they were also usually on those jobs.
(Hoffman 1996a)

Other families had similar stories. The Lemisch family controlled the Romanian klezmer business,[5] those from the Buki area of the Ukraine (between Kiev
and Uman) often hired violinist Berl Freedman, and Teplekers (from another
Ukrainian town) stayed loyal to clarinetist Itsikl Kramtweiss and cornetist
Nachman Grossman.[6]

Landsmanshaft connections made a big difference for immigrants in the
first wave who wanted to hear the dance music they had known from Europe; it
was not until the next generation that bandleaders became more or less interchangeable. By then, it was more common to simply specialize in "Jewish" music
or to stake out individual turf by catering to the relatively small Hasidic and
Orthodox communities, whose wedding dance and music traditions differed
greatly from those practiced at less Orthodox affairs.[7]

For immigrants, booking a band was often an informal matter. Early bandleaders simply rounded up the neighborhood or family klezmer clan, who played
with neither a contract nor a guaranteed fee:

Somebody would call my dad and say, "Listen, Spector, how about bringing some of the boys over. I'm having a party at my house." And he
would get a violinist—there was always a violinist—a trumpet player
and a clarinet player, and they would go out and play these places, guaranteed no money. And they'd put the fiddle case on the piano and people
would throw the money in for them to keep playing. They used to come
to the house at night after they would play to get their money.[8] (Spector
1997)

With the founding of the "Internatsionale Musiker Yunyon af Philadelfiya"
(International Musicians' Union of Philadelphia, a strictly Jewish union) in 1894
and the Philadelphia Musical Society (a general union) in 1903, this sort of engagement became less common, although it persisted in some form until the demise
of the last of the early immigrant klezmorim in the 1950s. Jewish wedding musicians were among the founding members of Philadelphia's general musicians'
union. For those who knew the Jewish repertoire, it was also easy to find lucrative work at Greek, Russian, Ukrainian, Polish, Gypsy, and many other kinds of
ethnic celebrations where Eastern and Central European music were in demand.[9]
While such parties posed few musical challenges for the musicians, other cultural differences did come into play. Morris Hoffman recalls his first experience
playing for Gypsies:

At Seventh and Snyder there was a hall called "New Auditorium" Hall, owned by Mrs. Cohen who later had the Savoy Plaza [on North Broad St.], and they had a lot of Gypsy affairs. For those, we used to get paid in advance, usually in gold. One day, a fight broke out,[10] and I saw the knives come out, and I started packing up my clarinet and, as I was tiptoeing out, a Gypsy got a hold of me. He said, "Where the hell are you going, get back in there—this ain't nothin'!" And we started in with the freyle-khs again, and everyone was dancing. . . . We went 'til three, four in the morning. (Hoffman 1996b)

It did not take long before musicians from outside the ancestral klezmer orbit, including many Italians from the south Philadelphia community, joined the ranks of the klezmorim, performing at Jewish celebrations and spending sum-mers at Jewish resorts in the Poconos (mountains sixty miles north of Philadel-phia), in the Catskills, or at the Jersey Shore.[11]

Many orchestra leaders of this generation had been trained in conservatories or military bands and found notation to be the most convenient way to transmit their repertoire to younger musicians. Folios from the early 1900s provide some of the earliest evidence for tracing the evolution of local musical preferences. These manuscripts are contemporaneous with the earliest available sources from the music's homelands in Europe. They provide valuable evidence of the conti-nuity of previously established musical traditions on this side of the Atlantic.

Wedding halls replaced Europe's homes and outdoor gardens as the venues of choice for celebrations of all types.[12] These halls ranged from simple one-story structures to relatively ornate ballroom-style facilities located in hotels. Phila-delphia's early Jewish wedding halls included the Ambassador in Strawberry Mansion (North Philadelphia), Garrett Hall at Eighth and Lombard (Center City), and the Traymore in South Philadelphia. One of the most popular early venues was Stanton Hall, located in the heart of South Philadelphia, on Federal St. between Third and Fourth. The Alexander family, immigrant musicians from Belarus, ran it very much like an Eastern European "wine garden," retaining old-world catering customs:

Before the restaurants, there were halls, where, if there was a wedding, there was no caterer; the bride's mother and an aunt, they did the cooking . . . and they would cook for weeks at a time. The family rented the hall. . . . The hall had long benches and long tables, and this is where they made the wedding. They didn't even hire waiters; they'd just pass the food around. The women would carry the pots in the sides of their aprons.[13] (Uhr 1998)

Informal wedding halls, such as the Stanton, gave klezmorim license to con-tinue the time-honored tradition of training young wedding musicians on the bandstand. Consequently, most bands consisted of four or five fairly well-paid seasoned wedding musicians along with an equal number of meagerly paid (or unpaid) apprentices. Morris Hoffman (born in 1912) describes his initiation into this world in the mid-1920s:

> Shulem [Sam] Alexander played the clarinet, except when his uncle Motl played [clarinet], in which case he played trombone. I learned by sitting next to him. Tulye (Naftule) Alexander played trumpet, and Joe Alexander played drums. Sam and Tulye owned the hall and booked all the work there, and their son Jack became a caterer. If you played the Stanton Hall, the Alexanders were always in the band. Shulem Alexander was business-minded. He was an entrepreneur, booking two jobs for himself at a time. So I would sub for him—I was 13, 14 years old when I used to sit in with them. He'd give me two or three dollars for the whole job. That's how I learned the repertoire.[14] (Hoffman 1997a)

As Jewish immigrants became more prosperous and learned more about American-style parties, old-style wedding halls gave way to catering halls, many of which doubled as restaurants. Uhr's Roumanian Restaurant (located at 509 S. Fifth St.) was a popular venue for Jewish celebrations from when it opened in 1930 until it was torn down in 1967. It was one of Philadelphia's first full-service Jewish catering establishments and often handled two or even three weddings at a time. It was a personalized, family-oriented business establishment that was closely connected to the community it served:

> The restaurant consisted of 144 seats, with second- and third-floor banquet rooms. Also, on the third floor we had our living quarters. The restaurant was located five blocks south of Independence Hall. We were in the heart of the #9 and the #50 trolley car [lines]. The Jews who were concentrated in Strawberry Mansion, Logan, and South Philadelphia would all have to pass our restaurant any time they went to visit their relatives in another neighborhood. . . . We also had fifty high chairs, because it was a family restaurant. I could tell you what time it was by who came in the door. The second and third floor originally were divided into rooms, and we decided to tear out the walls; that was how the catering business started. . . . In those days the linen was all white; nobody dyed it to match the color of the bride's eyes back then. (Uhr 1998)

While the bread and butter of the klezmer business was the wedding trade, musicians found many other occasions to perform their repertoire, including other life-cycle events and landsmanshaft gatherings (Uhr 1998). The Boslover Hall, built by immigrants from Boguslav in 1925 at Seventh and Pine Sts., was used by Jewish benevolent societies from various towns and cities for nearly forty years. Klezmorim also performed in synagogues, clubs (bars), "tea houses" (alcohol-free gathering places), and private homes.[15]

Some of those who could read music found their way into the pit orchestras of one of Philadelphia's early twentieth-century Yiddish theaters. By the turn of the twentieth century, these included the Germania (on Third St. near Girard Avenue), the Thalia (near Fourth and Calowhill), the Wheatley Dramatic Hall (at 511 South Fifth St.), the Market House Hall (at 735 Christian St.), and the Standard (at 1126–1134 South St.). In later years, the best known Yiddish theaters were the American Theatre at Franklin Street and Girard Avenue in Northern Liberties, Tomashevsky's Garden at Eighth and Race, and the Arch Street Theatre, located at 613 Arch St. in the neighborhood now known as "New City" (Boonin 1999).

The Arch Street Theatre, located in a building dating from 1828, survived longer than any other theater and is still well remembered in the community. It featured top New York and New York–bound productions, providing regular employment for some of Philadelphia's best Jewish musicians. These versatile players got to work with some of the Jewish music world's most skillful conductors and composers, including Jacob Musnitsky, Harry Kandel, Joseph Frankel, Sholem Secunda, and Joseph Schreibman.[16] Minnie Fryer, whose father Berl Freedman spent many years playing, arranging, and contracting for the Arch Street Theatre orchestra, recalls the camaraderie of the musicians who worked there:

> My father came over around 1905, to avoid serving in the Russian Army. Later, we brought my uncle Louis over, and he became the clarinetist at the theater. I remember that when the musicians would change their shoes to come into the pit and play, my uncle Louis would nail the shoes to the floor, just to see their reactions when they came back and tried to put them on. The musicians who worked in the theater had a wonderful sense of humor. (Fryer 1997)

The Arch Street Theatre was torn down in 1936.

In the early 1920s, Jewish musicians began to play on local Yiddish radio. Versatile reedman Morris Hoffman worked as a musician on these broadcasts beginning in 1929:

> Max Mosicant led the band on the Nathan Fleisher's Jewish hour, and his brother, Bennie, would write the arrangements. We'd play for local acts and bigger ones from New York. Freydele Oysher was a regular on that show along with her very famous brother, Moyshe [a cantor, actor, and film star]. We played everything on those shows, from opera to marches to patriotic songs. [Pianist] Joe Schreibman was a wonderful vocal accompanist. He used to lead the band on the Jewish hour on WPEN. On the vocal numbers I would play the cello parts on the baritone sax, and then I'd pick up my clarinet and play the freylekhs. (Hoffman 1997)

There were also opportunities for Jewish musicians to record their repertoire. Between 1917 and 1927, bandmaster Harry Kandel cut more than ninety
Jewish-oriented sides for the Victor Talking Machine Company,[17] whose main
studios moved to Camden, New Jersey (directly across the Delaware River from
Philadelphia), in 1924. Born in Krakow and classically trained at Odessa Conservatory, Kandel (1885–1943) emigrated to New York around 1905, going to
work as an assistant band director for John Philip Sousa and as a conductor on
the very popular Keith Vaudeville Circuit. Just before World War I, he relocated
to Philadelphia, becoming the bandleader at the Arch Street Theatre. His connections with Sousa helped him secure a recording contract with Victor, and his
theater pit orchestra became his recording orchestra (Rothman 1998).

Kandel's recorded output reflected the richness of Philadelphia's early
klezmer scene.[18] It included lively freylekhs brought by the Hoffmans from Kriovozer and Bagapolye, khusidls from the Freedman family, and other dance tunes
brought over by the Freeds, Swerdlows, and Alexanders from Belarus, along with
Kandel's own considerable repertoire. A twelve-inch wedding medley disk (circa
1918) featured radio personality Isidore Meltzer in the role of a badkhn, and
doynes showcased the extraordinary flute artistry of Israel Chazin and the virtuosic mallet playing of Jacob Hoffman.[19] Kandel's rendition of the Philadelphia
Russian Sher medley took up two sides of a 78 and included a variant of a sher
brought over by the Lemisch family in the late nineteenth century (for more on
this medley, see Chapter 5).

In his early recordings (1917–1922),[20] Kandel favored a brassy, military-
style sound. On them, some of the personalities from Philadelphia's early
Jewish music scene come to life, including the immaculately precise trumpeter
Sam (Shmilik) Portnoy, the consummate classically trained violinist Berl
Freedman, Belarus-born clarinetist and trombonist Sholem Alexander, accom-
plished tubist Morris Schnitzer, trombonist Charles Gusikoff (on loan from the
Philadelphia Orchestra where he later became principal trombone), and versa-
tile pianist Charlie Barron. Kandel's later work included jazzy novelties such as
"Jakey Jazz 'Em Up" (1926), a reworking of a popular Romanian bulgar that he
claimed was the inspiration for fellow Philadelphian Ziggy Elman's "Frailach
in Swing" (1939), later known in its vocal rendition as "And the Angels Sing"
(Rothman 1998).

While Kandel's recordings theoretically made Philadelphia's repertoire
available to the rest of the country, their content seemed to have little impact
elsewhere. Non-Philadelphian Jewish musicians tended to remain immersed in
their own traditions or copied the contemporaneous trends from New York
giants, such as Naftule Brandwein and Dave Tarras. Recordings of locally popular repertoire made by other Philadelphia Jewish bandleaders, including Itzikl
Kramtweiss, Abe Neff, and Marty Lahr, also had little national impact (and
probably little national distribution).

The musicians who were part of Philadelphia's Jewish wedding scene in
the 1920s and 1930s formed a community that had a life of its own. Pianist Jerry

Weinstein, the son of one of the stalwarts of that community, clarinetist Dave Weinstein, recalls the special camaraderie enjoyed by his father:

> It was a cultural connection for them. It was a meeting point, where everybody understood where everyone else was coming from. They had a common language in the Jewish music, and also stories, stories from the Old Country and from their lives here. They were friends as well as co-workers. It really was a brotherhood. (Weinstein 1997)

Indeed it was a brotherhood, but one not without its own hierarchies. A clear point of demarcation within the community was the tension, interplay, and perceived gulf between the klezmer, the vestige of medieval folklore, and the *muziker*, the classically trained mainstream Jewish musician who often carried on the klezmer music tradition while distancing himself from klezmorim. The contrast between these two Jewish musical archetypes grew increasingly pronounced beginning in the later decades of the nineteenth century when conservatory training became an option for Jewish musicians. As a result, a clear class distinction emerged between the more traditional hereditary musicians, who sought little beyond success in the party trade, and their more acculturated or conservatory-trained colleagues, who harbored other ambitions and craved a different sort of status. Such a split became fairly common, even within musical families and especially between fathers and sons. Morris Hoffman remembers the differences between the two generations that were active when he began his professional career in 1929:

> We were Americanized by the 1930s. On trumpet, the top players when I started were Jack Swerdlow, Sam Portnoy, Harry Chazin, Max Petrofsky, and Morris Grossman, but there were also the guys in the older generation, klezmers like Kotsky, Dave Finkelstein, Yoina, Jack's father, Meyer Swerdlow, and Morris's father, Nachman Grossman. The top clarinetists were Lou Lemisch, Dave Weinstein, and Jerry Adler; there were also klezmer clarinetists like Old Man Portnoy and Itzikl Kramtweiss. The popular violinists were Al Small, Bernie Berle [Bernie Gorodetzer], Max Essner [Jack Lewis] and Max Mosicant; at the same time there were still klezmer fiddlers: Sender, Itzy Krepke, Elias Cohen, and Moshe Mosicant, Max's father, who also played the saxophone. (Hoffman 1997)

In a world from which the badkhn quickly disappeared, klezmorim, or "klezmers" as they were called in the Philadelphia community, were a leftover European-style curiosity. Indeed, while many musicians active in the early to mid-twentieth century identified others as klezmorim, none whom I spoke with were willing to pin the label on themselves.[21] Cornetist Samuel Katz (whose brother Kalman, my grandfather, was considered a klezmer by many) articulated a few of the possible reasons for the younger American musicians' abhorrence of the label:

> A klezmer could only play the Jewish[22] music; they would have to hire kids like us to play the American repertoire. Itzikl Kramtweiss was typical of the old-timers. He'd point to a page with one flat in the signature and say, "What key is this?" and I'd tell him, "It's the key of "F," and he'd mimic me, "Key of "F!" Ha! He thinks he's so smart!" Several times, when I worked for him, he refused to pay me. I had to get him thrown out of the union.[23] (Katz 1980)

In the Jewish musical community, "American" players carried an aura of "normalcy" in contrast to the klezmers, who were commonly looked down on as suspicious outsiders, even back in Europe (see Chapter 1). Indeed, in the twentieth-century United States, where all musicians were somewhat marginalized, klezmorim carried a double burden, in that they were often considered pariahs within the Jewish musical community.

The "otherness" of the klezmer was very much a part of the early Philadelphia wedding music scene, and the exploits of some were quite consistent with folkloric European klezmer stereotypes, which pegged them as womanizers, gamblers, and swindlers who lived in their own idiosyncratic world. They also kept their distance by continuing to speak klezmerloshn, the secret argot that they refused to teach to outsiders,[24] particularly at times when prices were being negotiated or when the younger, more Americanized musicians were being paid.

In Philadelphia, the new generation of musicians usually referred to the klezmers by their nicknames, such as "Old Man Finklestein" (Dave Finklestein) "Old Bellow," and "Grossman the *Shiker*" (the drunkard; Nachman Grossman). Legends of these eccentric characters abound, including stories of Grossman playing the cornet nude in the *shvits* (ritual bathhouse) and old man Lemisch making dollar bills disappear up the bell of his clarinet. A klezmer named Mr. Morrison was well known both for his ability to play many instruments and his refusal to distinguish one from another. Morris Hoffman recalls a snowy night when he called Mr. Morrison to play bass:

> An hour later he showed up with a flute. He said, "Did you honestly expect me to lug a bass here on a night like this?" And he sat there and played the flute for the rest of the night. (Hoffman 1996a)

As in Europe, Jewish musicians played pranks on each other and did not hesitate to exact revenge when they thought it necessary.[25] Composer David Raksin recalls an often related anecdote about the coarseness of klezmer justice:

> There was a bass player, he played the tuba, his name was Schnitzer. There was a ballpark near where we lived, and we used to go there when-

ever possible, and he would sometimes play there with a little pickup band. And what happened was that he put down his tuba—it was an upright tuba, not a sousaphone—and he goes off to do something or other, and he comes back, and some sonofabitch had taken the remnants of a chicken, a roast chicken, and shoved it into the bell of his tuba. And he played a few notes, and he said in Yiddish, *Ota, dos iz nisht Schnitzer's ton.* Then he somehow found out who had done it, and he threw the mouthpiece at this guy, the mouthpiece of his tuba, and it hit him above the eye and opened a wound. (Raksin 1998)

As in Europe, those who were thought of as klezmorim often needed to hold down day jobs to get by; they worked as barbers, tailors, upholsterers, and in many other professions. In contrast, muzikers were often employed full-time in musical endeavors. Although they were largely conservatory trained, they seldom passed up the challenge of learning the newest popular styles. Jacob Hoffman, a virtuosic xylophonist who learned the entire Hasidic and klezmer repertoire from his father, began his light classical music career at age twelve, playing concert xylophone selections with Italian bands (Hoffman 1996b). Later, he performed many of the same selections on the Keith Vaudeville Circuit and also worked with the Philadelphia Orchestra and the touring companies of the Ballets Russes and the D'Oyly Carte Opera Company. Four descendants of the Gusikoff family (hailing from a long and distinguished line of klezmorim) found their way into the Philadelphia Orchestra (Gorodetzer 1998).[26]

It was not always clear where the line could be drawn between klezmer behavior and the general predilections of "club-date" musician culture. For example, many bandleaders became notorious for booking more work than they could handle and then farming the extra jobs out to others whom they trusted. Some were forthright about their need to subcontract bands, while others were less honest:

Joey Singer had six or seven guitars, and on any given Sunday he'd book himself six or seven simultaneous weddings. He'd make the rounds early in the day, setting up the stage, and in each hall he'd leave a guitar on one of the chairs. Then he'd go home. Inevitably, at some point the folks having the party would ask, "Where's Joey?" The answer was always the same: "I'm not sure where he went, but he couldn't have gone too far because his guitar's right here."[27] (Block 1999)

Sexual promiscuity also figured prominently in the popular lore concerning Philadelphia's Jewish musicians. In this anecdote, Morris Hoffman recalls a leader renowned both for his good looks and his sexual prowess:

One time the band assembled to play a wedding ceremony and nobody could find the leader. Finally, he comes prancing in, holding a stick with a condom tied around it. I ask him where he's been and he says, "I just fucked the bride."[28] With him that was only the beginning; once when we played for a ladies' auxiliary, he ended up bleeding so badly from the sex he had in the back room that I had to drive him to the hospital. (Hoffman 1999)

It is worth noting that, for a large number of Jewish immigrant musicians who came to Philadelphia, careers in Jewish music were the furthest thing from their minds. Many of these musicians were performers with symphonic aspirations, the most skilled of whom joined the fledgling Philadelphia Orchestra or one of the other permanent ensembles that performed for opera, ballet, or musical theater. Others found their way into vaudeville-house orchestras or motion picture pit bands[29] or found work in hotel, restaurant, and nightclub orchestras.

For the descendants of families who pursued such a path, even a "royal" klezmer heritage (such as that of the Gusikoffs) was usually not considered a proud one,[30] and in chronicling their family's legacy, they tended to privilege their forbears' performance of light classical repertoire for non-Jewish patrons instead of the Jewish aspects of their musical heritage. The recollections of Harry Gorodetzer, a fifty-year member of the Philadelphia Orchestra, provide insights into such attitudes, as well as into the "acculturation" that typically took place when ancestral klezmer families reached the Philadelphia area:

How far does music go back in my family? I'd rather not look back as far as the horse thieves. My grandfather, Berl Bas, played the bass. . . . He came from a small town in the Ukraine, Cherkas, not too far from Kiev . . . and (his orchestra) played for all kinds of affairs, for Jews and for non-Jewish royalty. My parents survived in Russia, even during the pogroms, because they needed my father as a musician, and they needed my mother as a midwife. (Gorodetzer 1998)

Next Gorodetzer looks to establish the family's credibility as classical musicians:

My father, Meyer, had studied classically in Warsaw. He also played in the Kiev opera as a young man. My parents came to Philadelphia around 1895, as did most of my father's siblings. By 1905, my father was running a music school at Fifth and Morris (in South Philadelphia). . . . He was a conductor, and tried to start a second symphony orchestra here in Philadelphia. (Gorodetzer 1998)

Having established his family's legitimate post-klezmer musical credentials, he switches to recounting the klezmer and popular side, which also endured in his family:

My uncle Motl was less of a highbrow. . . . he had two sons, Jacob who was a bass player, and Joe who was a damn good fiddle player; they did commercial work, not so much symphonic. . . . For example, you may know that Paul Whiteman was a viola player, but didn't play very well. One time he was here in Philadelphia, on TV, and Whiteman was moving his bow [with soap on it so it wouldn't sound] and it was really my cousin Joe playing backstage—it became pretty obvious to the viewers at one point when Joe stopped to sneeze and Whiteman kept moving his bow. (Gorodetzer 1998)

Finally, Gorodetzer tells how his own career fits in with his family legacy:

Anyhow, I joined the Philadelphia Orchestra in 1936 when I was twenty-one, and stayed for fifty years. My brother Sam played violin in the orchestra for twenty-five years. My brother Bernie [Berle] was a Jewish bandleader. I played with him occasionally, not the Jewish dance tunes, but Strauss waltzes and current jazz tunes that we all knew by ear. . . . My father had led the band at the Walnut Street Theater and also at the Graves Hotel, and we had all played with him, so we knew all kinds of music. (Gorodetzer 1998)

Gorodetzer's brother, Bernie Berle, died in the 1960s, but as one can tell from this account, there was a profound contrast between the bandleader and his brothers who were members of the Philadelphia Orchestra. Bernie Berle's family recalls the prestige of living with a man who was a favorite entertainer of local politicians and the darling of newspaper columnists while having to put up with the emotional abuse and violent tendencies of someone who, like generations of klezmorim before him, had no idea how to deal with children. Joe Borock remembered him this way:

Bernie Berle was a huge hulk of a guy, and he married this wonderful little Italian girl (Cora) who was around five-foot five. She would drive him everywhere and lug all the stands and music around. Danny Shankin used to talk about walking home from the union with him. He'd stop at the Reading Terminal market and buy scraps of food. When he got home the first thing he did was throw everything into a pot of boiling water. Then, when everything was cooked, his five kids would gather around him like puppies, and he'd throw the scraps of food into their mouths. . . . He was a tough guy. One time I remember walking into the union and he had another bandleader by the neck—I think it was your grandfather—had him up against the wall and he was screaming, "You don't take jobs away from me, take food out of my kids' mouths . . ." All he'd done was gotten a job that Bernie Berle was after.

But I really liked him—he had a wonderful wry sense of humor. (Borock 1999)

The division in such families actually had less to do with roots than with each individual's lifestyle choices and personal ambitions with regard to class status. In fact, many orchestral musicians of the time had spent their formative years playing folk and light classical repertoires by ear in family salon orchestras, like the one Harry Gorodetzer describes earlier. An anecdote from Bobby Roberts underscores the "family" relationship between Jewish wedding musicians and the orchestral players of his day:

> Many times I go to do a job with the Meyer Davis orchestra, at the Bellevue [the Bellevue-Stratford Hotel] or at a mansion, and at midnight the doorbell would ring and you'd see maybe a dozen violins come in joining the band, from the Philadelphia Orchestra! And, I'll tell you the difference between the musicians in those days and today: When you came to play with the Meyer Davis orchestra, you had your music to play, but when you start faking all the old society tunes, these guys were playing them like they were (nothing). . . . that's what you call talent. They could do anything—they could go out and join the klezmers and play freylekhs all night, and then the next day they'd be back with Stokowski! (Roberts 1998)

Accomplishment in other, more vernacular forms of American music also brought prestige. The Spectors were a multigenerational klezmer family from Kiev, with their Philadelphia branch headed by drummer "Hymie *der toyber*" (Hymie, the deaf one, so called because he could only hear out of one ear). One of his sons, Morris Spector, considered by many to be Philadelphia's premiere Jewish and popular music drummer, began work with Paul Whiteman in 1926 and was prominently featured on the first recording of Ferde Grofe's *Grand Canyon Suite*. Later, he became the drummer for Jan Savitt's well-respected Philadelphia-based jazz big band while also working clubs as a xylophone soloist. His brother, Max, who worked as a drummer with Savitt, Bunny Berrigan, Mitchell Ayres, and others, articulated the distinction between the klezmorim of his father's generation and American-style working musicians:

> We weren't klezmer as such. We were top-of-the-line musicians. We played the radio stations. . . . you had to be a top-notch musician to do that. . . . I was never out of work since the day I started at twelve years of age playing for strippers in a saloon at Sixth and Jackson. (Spector 1998)

Immigrant musicians arriving in Philadelphia in the 1920s joined the city's well-established Jewish musical families. Some found a comfortable home in the Jewish wedding scene, while others remained "greenhorns" for the duration of their careers. Volhinian-born clarinetist and flautist Dave Weinstein came to Philadelphia along with his brother, drummer Abe Weinstein, in 1923 after living for several years in Argentina. The two of them were sponsored by their sister Mary, who had already come to the United States and had married into a local musical family, the Goldsteins (this family would later produce bandleader Jackie Gold, whom we meet in Chapter 3). By the 1920s, the Jewish community, previously centered primarily in South Philadelphia, was beginning to disperse, and the Weinsteins settled in West Philadelphia. While living in Buenos Aires, they had picked up a large repertoire of tangos and semi-classical pieces that gave their band a cosmopolitan flair, especially when it came to playing a different kind of "dinner concert music" (Weinstein 1997). The brothers, having previously played in Europe, were veterans of European-style several-day weddings, so the late-night affairs in Philadelphia did not faze them in the least. They also brought memories of difficult years in Russia to a generation that only knew of the American experience, as recounted by Dave Weinstein's son Jerry:

> They were drafted into the Russian Army, and being musicians saved their lives . . . although my father remembered being caught by the Cossacks once and being beaten. Playing music got them through that. . . . Can you imagine what it was like for Jews to be drafted into that army, what a culture shock that must have been?[31] (Weinstein 1997)

When Dave Weinstein came to Philadelphia, he befriended Tevye Gorodetsky, a violinist with many connections on the hotel circuit, which led to lucrative summer bookings at resorts. During the 1930s, he worked occasionally as a concert flute and piccolo player with orchestras organized under the New Deal agency, the Works Progress Administration. Even though Weinstein was unschooled, he considered himself an artist and wanted to be perceived that way. Nevertheless, as his family grew he sought work closer to home, which landed him at Uhr's restaurant, where he became a regular with the Philadelphia stalwarts. Jerry Weinstein felt that, even in the mundane wedding grind, his father always kept a certain edge, never adopting the cynical attitudes endemic to many of the "outside" players:[32]

> I think he had a certain relationship to music that I didn't pick up from the other musicians he played with. From some of the other musicians, I got the feeling that this was a gig, it was a way to make a living, but for him, it had to do with his soul. This was a real expression of something that his whole identity was built around. When he was blind and old and could barely walk, and hardly had any energy, he would still practice. He practiced every day. (Weinstein 1997)

Perhaps the last "klezmer" on the Philadelphia scene was Dave Kantor, a musician from southern Ukraine who emigrated in the 1920s. Kantor, known throughout his career for his pencil mustache, was marked as a greenhorn on arrival and remained in that category for the rest of his life. When survivors came over from Eastern Europe after World War II, he became their primary choice for every party, performing with his wife, European-born singer Edith Lit. He was known for introducing himself to members of that community as Philadelphia's the preeminent Jewish entertainer as soon as they arrived in town. "The rumor was that he would grab them off the ship," said long-time Kantor sideman, trumpeter Chick Sherr (1997), who played with him starting in 1955 until Kantor's death in the mid-1980s:

> He used me and pianist Sammy Zager, and Morty Goodman was usu-
> ally the drummer. Dave did lots of Jewish—his clients wanted the real
> thing. They wanted the sher, they wanted the Romanian volakh. On the
> long medleys, we'd trade off on the melody—we called that a "dogfight."

Many of the American-born musicians found Cantor's old-world ways amusing. Drummer Bernie Weinstein recalls that Dave would often offer him a shot of whiskey at the outset of a job. "He'd say, 'Bernie, you wanna shnopsel? I gotta take one or two before a job. It gives me encouragement.'"

Kantor was a friendly man, but he retained traces of the European klezmer mentality, especially when it came to competition. When any of his sidemen booked work for themselves, he would stop using them. Bernie Weinstein (2007) remembers trying to find a way to get even with Kantor after being dropped as a sideman for competing with him:

> We're playing a small job one time and Dave's got a big job upstairs.
> So I saw him and said, "Dave, the funniest thing happened." "What's
> that?" he asked. "A well-built, good looking man of 90 years old came
> over to me in the bathroom and said, 'Do you know Dave Kantor?' I
> said, 'Of course I know Dave Kantor. He's a friend of mine.' And the
> man said, 'He played my Bar Mitzvah.'" "You're very funny, Bernie," was
> Dave's response.

Even though first- and second-generation American musicians liked to boast about their versatility, many harbored a soft spot for the Jewish wedding trade. Since the theaters and vaudeville houses where many of them worked were "dark" on Sundays, quite a few of these musicians stayed active on the Jewish circuit, which especially thrived on Sunday weddings.

Many musicians considered themselves Jewish bandleaders, but the scene was actually dominated by a handful of savvy individuals who truly knew how to work the local crowd. The four leaders who had become most established by the 1940s were Jack Lewis (Max Essner), Bernie Berle (Bernard Gorodetzer), Max Mosicant, and Al Small. In keeping with the European tradition, all were violinists. Bandleader Bobby Roberts speaks of the labeling that worked both for and against the "Jewish" leaders:

> All four could program a wide variety of popular and society music depending on the preferences of the individual client; still, within the music community and the general community, once you were identified as an "ethnic" leader, that label stuck with you throughout your career. (Roberts 1998)

These bandleaders were considered reliable professionals. They often worked in tandem with caterers, florists,[33] and masters of ceremonies, who performed a role reminiscent of Europe's badkhonim, the Jewish folk poets who enlivened celebrations as far back as the Middle Ages. It was the job of the master of ceremonies to announce the arrival of the guests, to run the various ceremonies,[34] and to lead the dancing if necessary; the full function of the leaders and emcees is discussed in Chapter 4. Some leaders received all of the work within their communities of origin (the *vayin* or landsmanshaft), assuring their knowledge of familiar repertoire for guests who originated from the same European towns. Others would advertise in the local Yiddish newspapers. Sometimes the calls came directly to specific leaders, who concocted ingenious ways of spreading their names around. Recalls Marvin Katz (1998),

> My father [Kol Katz] would have me scan the Jewish newspapers for engagement announcements, look up the addresses in the telephone directory, and send out a mazel tov [congratulations] along with his business card. I can't tell you how many jobs came in this way.

While caterers were prohibited by law from having "house bands," they were often called on to help plan the musical aspects of the party. They would usually rely on previous experience with a variety of leaders or, in some cases, funneled all of their work to one leader. As Bernie Uhr recalls, by the late 1920s Philadelphia's klezmer repertoire was mostly standardized, so that it hardly mattered which leader was hired:

> Years ago, you didn't need a named orchestra, because you weren't selling tickets to a dance. They wanted music. So if they looked to us, we would recommend Max Mosicant, Al Small, Lou Lemisch, and we liked these people, so we used to recommend them. We would call the orchestra leader and get a quote, and if they said it was on, it was on. There was no such thing as a contract between them and us. (Uhr 1998)

Once the booking was secure, each leader would need to find a band. It might be a set unit or a fairly random collection of freelancers who could function well together because of their common skills and repertoire. Many leaders contracted multiple groups on any given weekend day and night, keeping track of their engagements in large calendar books. The "American" Jewish bandleaders did all of their booking on Mondays and Thursdays at the Union Hall, located on N. Eighteenth St., where hundreds of musicians of all ethnic backgrounds gathered for "the meeting":

> Everything was done Mondays and Thursdays at the union. The leaders would come down, and if they didn't see who they wanted, there was somebody there with a megaphone who would page you, like, "Morris Hoffman," and I'd go to him, and the man who wanted to see me was right there. We'd settle the price, the time, the instrumental doublings, everything right there on the union floor. This was true for everyone except the big society leaders, Meyer Davis and Howard Lanin, who had offices and did everything by telephone.[35] (Hoffman 1999)

Veteran musician Joe Borock remembers that when he started teaching school he thought he could stop going to the union meeting, but soon enough, he came to regret his decision:

> The Thursday after Labor Day was the big day. . . . You could go down there and book most of your work until the first of the next year. When I got my teaching job about forty-five years ago, it was the first time I didn't go down to the union after Labor Day. I come home from school and the phone is ringing off the hook, and it's all the leaders calling, "Where were you? I have all these dates for you!" Anyhow, I told all of them I was sick of them and didn't need their stupid dates anymore. Then, two weeks later I got my first paycheck and I nearly fainted. I got back on the phone and tried to get my work back. . . . it took me years to recuperate from that. (Borock 1999)

As ancestral klezmer families diversified their portfolios, musicians from outside that orbit continued to jump in and pick up the work others left behind. For those from klezmer families who continued to focus their musical careers primarily on Jewish music, the repertoire became standardized. Certain families clearly had a dominant effect on that repertoire, especially the Lemisches, Swerdlows, and Hoffmans, whose members included talented composers, and in the Swerdlows' case, enterprising copyists. Morris Freed's sheet-music edition of the Philadelphia Russian Sher medley documented an early twentieth-century version of a tightly woven twenty-minute piece, profoundly different from the loosely improvised sher medleys performed in other cities (the Philadelphia Russian Sher is discussed at length in Chapter 5). Many of the bulgars and horas recorded by Kandel became standard fare, but only in Philadelphia. The community also had its share of klezmer-style composers, whose melodies quickly entered the mainstream and stayed there for many years.

The stock market crash of 1929 put a tremendous damper on the Jewish wedding music scene:

> The Depression killed a lot of the music. Excellent mechanics couldn't get jobs; engineers couldn't get jobs, so no one wanted to pay for music. We didn't get out of the Depression 'til we started preparing for World War ll. (Hoffman 1996c)

Still, for those who could afford it, the status quo of the 1920s continued throughout the 1930s. Then, in the early 1940s, many of the musicians in Hoffman's generation went overseas to fight or play in military bands during World War II. When they returned from the service, change was in the air, even in sleepy, provincial Philadelphia.

3

Philadelphia's Klezmer Tradition

The Later Years

The first decades after World War II brought a period of rapid expansion and significant change for the U.S. Jewish community. The move to suburbia created a need for new social institutions and resulted in the construction of an unprecedented number of new synagogues. It was also the era when Judaism entered the mainstream, taking its place next to Protestantism and Catholicism as a "normal" American religion (Wertheimer 1993: 6). The age of restrictive quotas directed against Jews was mostly over. Hotels and country clubs lifted their discriminatory barriers, and Jewish Americans found their way into new kinds of professional and academic careers and eventually into positions of political power. Historian Arthur Hertzberg sums up postwar Jewish aspirations as follows:

> They were numerous and increasingly wealthy, and ever more "Jewish". . . . they regarded the Jewish community as their primary home. Yet, they were deeply ambivalent, often without admitting it even to themselves, about their most Jewish emotions. . . . What they did as Jews—and more revealing, what they chose not to do had to fit their dominant purpose: to arrive. (Hertzberg 1989: 316)

The postwar period also marked a significant change in Philadelphia's Jewish wedding music scene. With the end of the war, the market became flooded with young and ambitious musicians who offered new ideas for entertainment that were often in sharp contrast to the time-worn ethnic formulas of their predecessors. They formed new groups, some of which were Jewish offspring of the Lester and Howard Lanin and Meyer Davis society orchestras that had established themselves in Philadelphia in the early 1930s.[1] These outfits offered new options for the Jewish party host, including Latin dance instruction and continuous music. Some orchestras discarded the older European ethnic repertoire altogether, replacing it with more contemporary Israeli fare.

Musical choices in the postwar era were a reflection of a larger phenomenon. While assimilation had affected many aspects of immigrant and first-generation American Jewish culture (language, business practices, housing choices), weddings and bar mitzvahs had stood out as symbolic bastions of immigrant identity and expression. In the new era the children of immigrants had a choice: They could have an old-world celebration with an American twist, or an American celebration with a brief nod to their Jewish roots.

Indeed, many musicians attribute the shift that occurred in the choice of wedding music to the increased power of the second-generation bride, who was not willing to allow her parents to dictate the character of her wedding celebration. Morris Hoffman describes how the tension of this era was played out at one party:

> The bride came over to talk to the band. "Please," she said. "I work with Gentile girls and my boss is Gentile. . . . No Jewish music!" So we started off with "Where or When," "Cocktails for Two," typical popular stuff. So the old man comes over and says, in Yiddish, "Why don't you play any Jewish music?" The leader tells him what his daughter said and he becomes furious. "How can you listen to that little *pishiker*? Play a freylekhs!" She came back over to protest and he called her every Jewish curse under the sun. And for the rest of the night the band played Jewish. (Hoffman 1996b)

The older generation kept the Jewish bandleaders in business, hiring them not only for family affairs but also to entertain at landsmanshaft and B'nai Brith (Jewish fraternal organization) parties and to play for social clubs. The new generation of musicians who began working for these bandleaders in the 1940s inherited a tradition that, while hopelessly archaic, was still surprisingly viable. Most of them were brought into the klezmer world as ringers: At heart, many of them were actually boppers, and left to their own devices, they would probably be jamming on Charlie Parker or Dizzy Gillespie tunes. Yet they could play the American dance tunes that the old-timers still could not handle, and they picked up the traditional tunes on the bandstand or read them from folios.

Clarinetist Joe Borock got into the Jewish wedding scene just after World War II, stepping in as an "American-style" ringer in bands made up of older players. His musical background is somewhat typical of the post-klezmer generation. After early training at Philadelphia's most prestigious music trade high school (Mastbaum), Borock became a regular auxiliary clarinetist in the Curtis Institute Orchestra. By 1937 at the age of fifteen, he also began work as a lead alto player in swing bands, and by the age of seventeen he was on the road playing one-nighters with the "name" big bands of Ray McKinley and, later, Charlie Barnet. After a stint in the service (where he played in a top Navy band) he came back to Philadelphia to play full time with local theater orchestras. By this time, his repertoire was well developed:

> I could play Goodman-style swing clarinet, and every dance band used four saxophones, but one of them had to be a jazz clarinet player. If you played nightclubs, you played the dance part and you played the shows— you had to read. Then, when you did society work, you had to know every tune from every show. (Borock 1997a)

His Jewish music career began in 1945 when he was working six nights a week at a popular night club, the Coronet:

> By this time the brides had gotten control of their own destiny, and they demanded American music. We were always off on Sunday nights, and that was a prime night for Jewish weddings. One of the Jewish leaders took a liking to me and heard that I knew American music, so he hired me. Now, I had already played with almost every Jewish leader in town and I didn't like klezmer music, but as I later found out it was because the guys I had learned it from were playing it all wrong. Most of the trumpet players were Italian, and there was something missing in their playing but I couldn't tell what; they played well but they really didn't play klezmer. Then I met Danny Shankin and Zeftie [Morris Zeft] and they played real klezmer with a lift, with a swing . . . you can't describe it. And they didn't use any music, although I did have Harry Swerdlow write a book for me. (Borock 1997a)

When Borock started his klezmer career there were still occasional old-world–style engagements for groups of Yiddish-speaking immigrants:

> Ninety percent of our work was weddings, and then there were the bar mitzvahs, which combined the ideas of mitzvah (commandment) and a bar. Once in a while, though, Danny would get other jobs. For example, I once reported to a job in the back room of Uhr's; he had a snare drum and I played the clarinet. There were a big bunch of guys in their shirt-sleeves and they had a barrel of shmaltz herring and jugs of whiskey, *balegoles* (wagon drivers) having a party. (Borock 1997a)

Joining the Jewish wedding scene in the 1940s, Borock also saw his share of old-time klezmer business practices.

> The older bandleaders would always bring their sons, and during dinner they played for tips. As soon as the dinner was over they'd give them a

dollar and say, "Good boy, go home!" So the kids would leave and then the leader would put the fiddle case in front of the band, and they wouldn't play unless someone put money in the fiddle case. (Borock 1997a)

For an American musician of Borock's generation, the sensibilities of the immigrant generation seemed totally foreign. He recalls receiving a request for a *drushegeshank*, a kind of announcement of a monetary wedding gift typical at European weddings, but, as far as he was concerned, totally out of place at American ones:

> Once we were playing downstairs at Uhr's, all scrunched together by the door, and the mother and father of the bride come up, and they say, "Joe, I want you should make an announcement. I want you should tell everyone that I'm giving my daughter and my new son-in-law their present—a hundred dollars!" So I said, "No, no, it would be nicer if you announced it." And the two of them stood there with grins on their faces. These people didn't know any better. . . . I was waiting for someone to come up and announce they were giving them a chicken or something. (Borock 1999)

Having been raised Orthodox in a small rural Jewish community,[2] Borock was constantly amused at the hypocrisy of Philadelphia's hard-pressed religious establishment:

> One time we were working downtown Uhr's,[3] and the caterer sees me and he says, "Joe, Come 'ere! Put on this coat and hat!" So I said, "What are you doing?" And he tells me that the rabbi, a very Orthodox rabbi, was doing the *ketubah* (signing of the nuptial vows), and needed a *gute yid* (pious Jew) to witness the thing, see, and they didn't have a *gute yid*. So I went in dressed like that, and I said "*Nu, Rebbe, vus . . .* (Yes, Rabbi, what do you need?)." So I did it. Later I found out that on other occasions he had sent his dishwashers in, decked out the same way. (Borock 1999)

Borock also remembers the challenge of playing the occasional religious wedding in which the hosts seemed completely out of touch with local customs. In such a case, he had no qualms about playing a subversive role:

> I remember that once I was booked for a four-hour wedding where they wanted nothing but Jewish music. The contractor went up to New York and got a big book of Hasidic songs, which we all had to read because none of us knew any of them. And people were grumbling, and I went over to the main table and spoke to the mother of the bride, who was paying and I said, "You know, you're ruining your party," and her husband said, "Never mind! No English!" Anyhow, so the dinner's over, and we're just

playing more freylekhs so I said, "To hell with it!" and I went into an American dance number, and the guests roared "Hooray!" Oh, well . . . (Borock 1999)

The Jewish repertoire of the late 1940s was but a shadow of the diverse corpus that preceded it. By examining several volumes notated in the 1940s and discussing the repertoire of that era with surviving musicians, I found that very few klezmer genres were passed on to the 1940s generation. Instead, folios from that time contain mostly bulgars and freylekhs,[4] along with more current Yiddish theater hits. By this time, a large variety of Latin dances were also included, along with "Palestinian" repertoire (which became "Israeli" in 1948); a healthy sampling of ethnic dances from outside the Jewish realm, including Irish, Italian, and Greek dances; and a few mummers' reels, a local specialty. New York's klezmer repertoire became known in Philadelphia through secondhand sources; casually transcribed variants of this tradition remain in Philly's vintage klezmer books, mistakes and all.[5]

A comparison of Philadelphia's klezmer repertoire with that of New York in the same period reveals the profound conservatism of Philadelphia's musicians. Few drummers used sock cymbals (or "hi-hats"), preferring to play mostly on the snare, Russian Army style. While innovative New York musicians such as Dave Tarras, Sammy Musiker, and Max Epstein experimented with chromaticism and jazz harmonies, their Philadelphia counterparts tended to rely on old standbys; even the composers worked completely within traditional boundaries. Standard klezmer volumes published in New York were still useless to Philadelphia's aspiring Jewish dance musicians, who had no choice but to buy handcopied tune books from local union copyists. New York klezmorim, coming mainly from other European towns and other family dynasties, had synthesized their own klezmer blend, as had musicians in Boston, Milwaukee, and elsewhere.[6] Philadelphia musicians' knowledge of "supplementary" material often placed them in high demand once they moved to New York.[7] Trumpeter Bernie Greenbaum (1999) remembers his first Jewish gig after he moved: "When I started playing things in New York, they didn't know any of the things that I played in the way of bulgars, having learned in Philadelphia, whereas I didn't know any of the Hasidic things that they were playing in New York."

Bobby Block, who is still active in Philadelphia at the time of this writing, was typical of the younger musicians who entered the Jewish wedding scene in the early 1950s:

My clarinet and sax teacher, Lou Orkin, wrote me my first Jewish book, and Berl Freedman and Charlie Barron also wrote a few things out for me. When you got a guy to write a book for you in those days, it was maybe a dozen freylekhs, the polka, the Russian Sher, a *kamarinska*, a *kozachok,* and then, not cha-chas or mambos, because this was before that, but they would write you a half-dozen rhumbas, a couple sambas, you had to have that in the back of the book. If you had a book like that you were in business. (Block 1997a)

By the time Block came on the scene, the audience was even more elderly, and he started out playing at what one might call a "Jewish nostalgia" club:

I played at a little club called the Pine Plaza at Fifth and Pine . . . and that was nothing but Yiddish music. After the Second World War, a lot of Jewish people who had made money would want to go out on a Saturday night. They were immigrants and this was a great place to go, a lot like Sammy's Romanian Restaurant in New York . . . these people didn't go to the regular nightclubs, like the Latin Casino, or to any of the musical bars. They wanted to hear Jewish music. They were kind of affluent. The Second World War was over, they'd made a lot of money during the war, so this was the kind of place they went to spend a few bucks. You'd have a steak, you'd have a *shnaps* (whiskey), they had a little band, they had an emcee, a guy named Abe Alemar. He was a modern emcee. (Block 1997a)

Alemar had been a popular Jewish radio host since the 1930s. His generation passed their version of Jewish entertainment on to the younger musicians, much as the klezmers had passed the tradition on to younger players in the 1920s and 1930s. Here Block describes how he got the engagement and learned the routines:

My drummer's father was a patron of the Pine Plaza. So he asked, "Why don't you let my son and his friends come down and play?" We had just gotten out of high school, but I guess he felt obliged since Mr. Shinder brought a whole crowd in every Saturday. He went up to the leader of the group and said we're gonna let these kids come in and play. And the leader was a guy named Charlie Barron. He used to play at the Arch St. Theatre. . . . I'm sure he must have groaned when he heard the news. So we came in there one night, we sat down, I didn't know how to blow my nose, much less blow my horn. And little by little we started to learn this Jewish music. We ended up staying there for three years. (Block 1997)

The scene at the Pine Plaza was a provincial throwback to the immigrant world of the 1920s. Block describes a typical show:

We got to know the routine. It was Charlie, Joel Shinder, myself, and Abe Alemar. We had a couple named Al and Lil Lewis. They sang—I can remember introducing them, "Ladies and Gentlemen, the stars of Yiddish Stage and radio, Al and Lil Lewis." And they'd come out and sing "Shalom, Shalom Bayis, Shalom Bayis do the Sholom Bayis . . ." A little cornball thing. We played every Saturday night, 9–2. We would get

$12 a piece, and we had a pitcher on top of the piano that people would put money into. If we ended up with $20 each for the night, boy, that was a good night. And we played great music, not just the freylekhs but the Yiddish theatre tunes that I never get to play any more. (Block 1998)

If Charlie Barron's bandleading style was a throwback musically, his style of doing business also harkened back to the days of the immigrant bandleaders. Block tells how one of Philadelphia's most popular freylekhs got its name:

Pasey was a patron at the Pine Plaza, and he would come in every week and he always wanted this melody. Well you know these things don't have names, so anyhow he'd give us a dollar or two. So one night Charlie Barron said to him, "You know, Pasey, you ought to buy this freylekhs. Give us ten dollars and it'll be your freylekhs, and everyone will know that it's Pasey's freylekhs. So he gave him a ten-dollar bill and from that night on that was Pasey's freyleksh. And all over the city everyone still calls that tune "Pasey's freylekhs." (Block 1998)

For the Jewish leaders who played weddings and bar mitzvahs, the scene began to change radically in the 1950s. In a 1998 interview Bobby Block sums up this new attitude: "That first American generation that became a little more affluent started to put down what the old people liked. They started joining country clubs and doing the cha-cha instead of the freylekhs. Soon the old music started to carry a stigma."

Some of the older bandleaders actually went and took cha-cha lessons, but for others, the new era presented an insurmountable challenge. "They thought these new dances were only a craze. Someone would request a cha-cha, so they'd play a rhumba. They all thought that after a few months the whole thing would be over and the freylekhs would be back in style" (Block 1998).

One powerful catalyst for a new approach was Bobby Roberts (1912–2001), a contemporary of many of the old-timers, he decided to veer off in the "society" direction and offer his clients a different kind of Jewish party. A veteran of the old Jewish wedding scene and of the Davis and Lanin society orchestras, Roberts knew firsthand how distinctly different the styles of leading orchestras could be, and he liked the model that Davis and Lanin offered:

Davis didn't bother with the union "meeting"—he ran his band out of an office. He dressed impeccably, but he never walked through the crowd, like the old-style leaders, who were always looking to shmooze for their next gig—in fact you never could figure out how he got to the bandstand. And when a job was over, Meyer simply disappeared— no shmoozing. If people wanted to book him, they would call his office. (Roberts 1998)

Roberts had become bored with what he thought of as musical stagnation in the Jewish repertoire and indignant about many of the old leaders' corrupt and outdated business practices. In a 1998 interview he assessed the old-style Jewish music scene, beginning with his view of the klezmers:

> They knew what they knew, and that was all. That was really the slop of your business. . . . If they knew it was a bad season, one of these guys might call you and say, "I got a job for you Saturday; it's only a small job—it only pays six dollars for a couple hours. He might be getting twenty-five for you, but he would *schnor* [cleverly swindle] you for money. A lot of the Jewish leaders would *schnor* the hell out of you. They didn't know how to dress—they'd show up in work clothes half the time. Also, they didn't even look at the crowd. During dinner they'd play dance music. And every wedding was the same. The younger leaders were different. Some of them, like Max Mosicant and Abe Neff, were real gentlemen. (Roberts 1998)

A big fan of Latin music and culture, Roberts had picked up a diverse and exotic Latin repertoire during the war, having met Cuban dancers on passes to Mexico while he was stationed in Texas. Returning to Philadelphia, he worked briefly with Abe Neff, the most assimilated of the old-school Jewish leaders,[8] who hired him to teach some Latin dancing at a wedding. Quickly realizing how lucrative it might be to go into business for himself, Roberts decided to start a Jewish-oriented booking agency that specialized in contemporary American-style party packages.

Throughout his career as a leader, he prided himself on his positive relationship with his clients. He recalled the engagement that led him to his later successes:

> It was 1948 and I got a call from Jack Lewis. He said, "I got a job for you; it's a trio out in Wynnefield (at the time, a mostly Jewish neighborhood), a private home, five to eight and here's the price of the job, and the guy will send me a check." I said, "Jack, I want to get out of this business, I don't want to play anymore. But who's on it?" He told me, "I got a guy named Lou King, he works steady at the Embassy (a popular restaurant at Broad and Locust), and I got a bass player for you, and that's it." So we went to the house, and Lou King comes in and introduces himself, and we played a set and took a break around a quarter to six. And then when the next set would have been over I went over to the host and said, "Listen, every time we stop I have to build up the crowd again. For an extra fifty bucks, we can keep playing continuous." And he said, "Sure, I like what you're doing, my daughter's happy, go ahead." (Roberts 1998)

Roberts went on to describe how he built what would have been a three-hour party into an all-night event that would have satisfied even the most resilient old-world Moldavian crowd:

> So we do, and I come up to him at a quarter to eight, and he says, "You're doing great!" And I say, "Well, we're supposed to quit in fifteen minutes, but I think I should keep playing; it ain't gonna be very expensive, I'll [keep track of the hours] on your bill." And he says, "You're making my daughter happy, the crowd's going crazy, keep on playing." About ten o'clock the bass player runs out of steam, I send him home. Lou says, "I'm fine; I don't quit!" So it goes on like that, and at five o'clock the host says, "Okay, the guests are leaving, just give me the bill; I don't care how much it is! You played Italian, Jewish, French, everything." So from then on Lou and I always worked together. (Roberts 1998)

In challenging what he thought of as the tired, outmoded format of the standard Jewish wedding, Roberts inadvertently stumbled on a perfect formula for an "American" party, a formula he had picked up not from old-country Jewish leaders, but from the Davis and Lanin orchestras. Roberts realized that he could offer a level of service beyond what the people expected from the popular leaders of the day. Along with another American bandleader, Jay Jerome, he formed a company that he called "Music Associates," and soon they had virtually cornered the Jewish market. By the mid-1950s, he was sending out more than twenty-six bands, all "client-friendly" and each with its own specialty:

> We made the business more respectable. . . . We knew, if we got to another city, we'd need tips for the porters—we weren't going to shlep our instruments, so we'd put it on the bill. We'd charge for transportation. We'd never let the client charge the band for food. We took care of everything. And our bands were like a franchise—the leader got a percentage of the gross—they knew they wouldn't get that elsewhere. (Roberts 1998)

The Roberts organization also influenced clients' expectations concerning the repertoire at Jewish weddings. Bandleader Marty Portnoy remembers this era of transition:

> When I got into the business [1947] the music you played was seventy-five percent Jewish, twenty-five percent English. When the cha-cha came out, it all of the sudden became fifty percent Jewish and fifty percent English because twenty-five percent was now cha-cha. As the years went by it just dissipated; it wasn't the most important thing at the affair. At one time you had to play the Jewish music or you weren't a bandleader, you weren't a musician. I remember playing with Al Small, and when the

older guys saw a young guy coming in, they would pick the most obscure Jewish song that there was, and then they'd go, "Okay kid, and you'd look at them, "Uh . . . uh . . ." (Portnoy 2000)

Despite the change in repertoire, the sense of the Jewish wedding music scene as a brotherhood carried over to the 1960s generation of bandleaders:

We had more fun on jobs in those days amongst ourselves. We would kibitz and play and do crazy things. We'd play a couple of wrong notes here and there, and we'd cover them up, but everyone would be cracking up all night. (Portnoy 2000)

Some other bandleaders took the idea of fun to the extreme:

We were at Temple Judea, Broad and Stenton. We're playing where the people sit, and nobody's sitting there, they're out on the floor, and up on the stage, they've got a couple of those horses with planks on them, they've got those big palms all around it, and there's a bicycle on the stage, and there's some Jewish books. We finally had an intermission and I go up on the stage, and I lay on the boards on the sawhorses. . . . They take the palms, put them all around me, one guy picks up the prayer book and reads from it like I'm dead, another guy takes the bicycle and rides it around, you had to be there to see it, you coulda dropped dead laughing—people were going crazy. (Weinstein 2007)

Of course, women were also part of the scene, although, in Philadelphia, nearly all of them were vocalists. One of the best and most enduring band singers is Gerri Dean. Born Geraldine Shmiegel, Gerri got into the business when clarinetist and bandleader Jerry Adler, a neighbor of hers in the Logan section of Philadelphia, heard her sing. "I used to wash the dishes in the evening, and he used to hear me through the window as I washed the dishes," she recalls. "I was about fourteen years old and he comes knocking at my door and says, 'I need someone to sing a wedding ceremony,' and I said, 'I don't sing that; I only sing blues'" (Cohen 1997).

That was not entirely true. Gerri's father was a cantor from Eastern Europe, well renowned for his compositions and choral arrangements. Her sister knew the entire Yiddish theatre repertoire on the piano, and her brother sang and played the violin. As a child in the 1930s, Gerri had wanted to join her father's choir, but he would only allow men to sing in it. Accepting that offer from Jerry Adler, she learned the three major staples of the American wedding ceremony ("Oh, Promise Me," "Because," and "I Love You Truly") and began her new career.

Soon enough, she had mastered the Yiddish repertoire of the time: "*Oy Mama, Bin Ikh Farlibt*" (Oh Mother, Am I in Love), "*Ikh Vill Zikh Shpiln*" (I Wanna Play), "*Vus Du Vilst, Dos Vil Ikh Oykh*" (What You Want, That's What

I Want), *"Sheyn Vi Di L'vone"* (Beautiful as the Moon), and many others. When the musicians would need a break during a twenty-minute Russian Sher, she would sing *"Der Neyer Sher"* (The New Sher). Meanwhile, she took on the entirety of the American songbook and party repertoire, later adding in rock, Latin, and rhythm and blues. When the Israeli Hebrew repertoire entered the scene, that became her new specialty. Ever the chameleon, she sang it like a sabra (native-born Israeli) and earned herself a spot in Philly's top Jewish party band, the Jules Helzner Orchestra.

When Philadelphia's Conservative rabbis passed an edict banning live music at Friday night bat mitzvah and Saturday afternoon bar mitzvah celebrations, they left a loophole that was very good for her business and for that of many of Philadelphia's other female vocalists: You could still hire a singer, as long as he or she performed solo. Gerri learned to teach party games, run a candle-lighting ceremony, lead dances (including Israeli dances, the "Bunny Hop," and the "Alley Cat") while singing, "as if I were a full orchestra!"

With the society model taking over, the older Jewish leaders eventually found themselves playing at fewer and fewer private parties, although they could still work landsmanshaft and B'nai Brith functions and at hotels and clubs that catered to the older set. Yet the younger leaders also had a problem, because they were reluctant to draw from the cadre they had grown up with in the business:

> You'd have musicians who were great with the Jewish, but they didn't know the cha-chas or bossas; they didn't know the English music. So it became very, very difficult. You had to get your own select guys. I picked certain people and we all grew together. . . . Then, as the years went by it reversed itself. Now you had guys who knew the American but didn't know the Jewish. (Portnoy 2000)

Still, when they played for their traditional audience, Philadelphia's surviving Jewish musicians held onto their repertoire, staying remarkably faithful to their roots. Unlike New York's musicians, who phased out their klezmer repertoire when most of their engagements became Hasidic functions, due to a large influx of Hasidim after World War II, Philadelphia's musicians had no choice but to take the klezmer and Yiddish nostalgia route. Many of these musicians still display a strange mixture of self-deprecation and pride when discussing their days with the "Jewish" bandleaders.

Despite the decline of Philadelphia's more traditional Jewish wedding scene in the 1960s, a variety of musical options remain for the Jewish party planner even today. As in many places, klezmer revival bands have emerged, giving the remaining society bands and old-style Jewish bands a good deal of healthy competition.

For the mainstream Jewish society bandleaders, Jewish music has been dead for many years, and it remains dead. For all practical purposes, the community that these bandleaders serviced has succumbed to the acculturation identified by sociologist Marshall Sklare (1959, 1967, 1974) in his landmark studies of suburban Jews in the 1950s. They have adopted a "selective" attitude toward their ethnicity, so that it does not in any way threaten their societal status. Bandleader Marty Portnoy, who came up in an era when Jewish repertoire was a substantial part of any engagement, including society affairs, sums up the frustration many leaders of his generation feel when working for such clients:

> At this point it's mostly rock 'n roll with some American standards. I find that there's very little Jewish music being played. If you get to play two numbers in an affair you're doing good—you're one over the limit. I've also been to many affairs where they've had a nine-piece band, including four singers who dance and perform routines. That's the current model, but I can't see thinking of a group like that as a band. There is no resemblance between that and what we used to do. (Portnoy 2000)

While ritual ceremonies are still part of many parties, they have, by and large, taken on a new character that differs radically from that of those held at earlier events. The lack of Jewish content in these ceremonies is perhaps a reflection of the low level of identification with the traditional content of Jewish celebrations, especially Jewish music, on the part of the clientele who throw society-type parties. It is also indicative of a younger generation of Philadelphia bandleaders (those active in the past thirty years or so) who have no awareness of or interest in the city's Jewish wedding music heritage. This disregard of tradition can be irritating to older bandleaders. Marty Portnoy sizes up one such contemporary ceremony:

> The people today who are leading bands unfortunately do not know how to do a ceremony. . . . they play rock 'n roll music for a crowning ceremony, which offends me very much. I was at one such affair recently. They did a candle-lighting ceremony, and called up the grandfather while they played "It's A Wonderful World." When they called the grandmother they played "Another One Bites the Dust." The other grandmother came up and they didn't know what to do, so they played some kind of blues riff. They just played anything that came into their minds. (Portnoy 2000)

Caterer Bernie Uhr sums up the contrast between the new and old style of celebration in particularly poignant terms:

> Years ago when you did a ceremony, the band would play a freylekhs to bring the grandfather up to light a candle. The bandleader knew what freylekhs was the grandfather's favorite. And the grandfather wouldn't just walk up to the candle; he'd dance his way up. This is all lost. (Uhr 2000)

Other current bandleaders who perform at Jewish functions may not even know the most fundamental rituals of a Jewish celebration:

> Pete Cole is an Italian fellow who was just starting in the Jewish field. He's an excellent musician—he plays trumpet and sings just like Tony Bennett. I had him booked over at Merion caterers for a Jewish affair, and the family walked over to him, they said to him, "We're gonna do the *Motzi*" [the blessing for the bread, which one must say at a Jewish celebration before any food is consumed]. So he says to himself, "The *Motzi*." He files it away and then they come back and say, "We've gotta do the *Motzi*." He still doesn't have a clue. So he says, "To hell with it." Now this was at the time when "The Hustle" was all the rage. So he calls it, and in the place where you usually stop and yell "Do The Hustle," he yells, "Do the *Motzi*." (Portnoy 2000)

Another popular former leader, Jackie Gold reflects on the circumstances that convinced him to leave the music business thirty years ago:

> I realized there was no way that I could keep up with the new popular tastes. For me it was a simple matter of mathematics. When I got into the business, I was twenty-two and the bar mitzvah boy was thirteen. Later on, I was forty and the bar mitzvah boy was still thirteen. Then I was fifty. . . . I was getting older, and less and less interested in what the younger people thought of as party music. When the Beatles came in, we all had to hire guitarists. These guys would drive up to the job on their Harleys, come in wearing blue jeans and sneakers, and get more attention from the crowd in five minutes than we got the entire night. Finally, I decided I'd had enough. (Gold 2000)

Others simply rolled with the punches. Bandleader Jules Helzner's career reads like a flexible mirror of the twentieth-century Jewish musical experience. Born in Russia in 1918, he came to Philadelphia when he was three, working almost immediately as a street musician who performed vaudeville hits on the street using a comb and tissue paper. By the time he reached high school, he had mastered the clarinet and saxophone and formed a band with his brothers, pianist Maury (later the celebrated director of Philadelphia's Workmans Circle Chorus) and drummer Abe. Soon he was in demand from the older Jewish bandleaders, including Max Mosicant (in fact, Helzner remembers performing with Mosicant's European-born father), Al Small, and Jack Lewis. "I copied everything Dave Tarras did on the clarinet" (Helzner 2006), but for Helzner it did not end there; he also copied every major clarinet and saxophone innovator in swing, bebop, and rock 'n' roll, priding himself on his nonjudgmental versatility and adaptability. When Philadelphia's famed Victorian Amusement Park wanted to update its image to attract a younger crowd, it was Helzner who wrote and recorded for them its rock jingle, "Life Is a Lark at Willow Grove Park." Ever the innovator, he also received numerous awards for his life-saving humanitarian efforts as a ham radio operator.

From Klezmer Kings to Klingon Klezmers

Helzner's mercurial career represents the natural evolution of a twentieth-century Jewish society bandleader. By definition, society bands represent a type of musical organization whose repertoire is solely based on the tastes of a clientele who want their parties to project a wealthy, upper class image (MacLeod 1992: 4). It is only natural that the leaders of such bands would need to tailor their styles to contemporary tastes. For bandleaders with less of a society image, especially those who cut their teeth catering to the more ethnically oriented elements in the community, the revival of klezmer music created the possibility of an alternative—the opportunity to market a wedding or celebration that reflected the fun and spirit of the old days, before contemporary models took hold. One Philadelphia bandleader who proudly jumped at the opportunity to reintroduce the old Jewish tunes to his music book was Bobby Block, whose group, The Klezmer Kings, still performs a nostalgic mix for seniors and anyone else who will listen at about twenty-five engagements each year:

> It's only a small part of my bookings, but a part that I enjoy. There was certainly a time thirty-five or so years ago that I stayed away from this stuff, because people made fun of you if you played it. "Jewish music?" they'd say. "What, you play weddings and bar mitzvahs?" I thought it was a shame. My parents went to the Yiddish theater every week when I was a kid. Those songs meant a lot to me, and I still sing them. Anyhow, the attitudes all changed about twenty years ago when younger people started playing the music. (Block 1997)

Currently in his early seventies, Block struggles to find musicians who still remember enough of the older material to make his group authentic, but he definitely enjoys his role, pleasing a clientele that felt abandoned for many years:

> I play for the remaining landsmanshaft groups, the older congregations, certain B'nai Brith lodges, the Workman's Circle folks. I live to see the joy on the faces of the older people. These aren't the folks with the accents and the broken English—that generation is gone. These are their children who remember their parents and the joy of traditional celebrations. (Block 1998)

However, Block's upbeat attitude is far from the norm. For most players of the older generation who moved on to other musical realms, participation in the contemporary klezmer scene can still carry a stigma. Elaine Hoffman Watts, daughter of mallet virtuoso Jacob Hoffman and current bearer of the torch for the Hoffman family klezmer tradition, relates a recent telephone conversation with retired studio trumpeter Mel Davis, whose experience as one of master clarinetist Dave Tarras's top sidemen did little to temper his well-worn attitude. "I call him and tell him about how exciting Klezkamp was, about playing with Howie Leess and Paul Pincus,[9] and he says to me, 'Elaine, you're a Curtis graduate, you're a fine musician, and you want to be a klezmer?' "[10] (Watts 2001, pers. comm.).

While Watts is exactly the same age as Block, I tend to group her with the klezmer "revivalists." This is because of her frequent affiliations with younger, creative-minded players (such as her daughter, trumpeter Susan Watts) and because, as a female drummer, she has had to wait for the gender-neutral revival to get any work on the Jewish scene at all.

The klezmer revival or revitalization movement (mentioned in the Introduction), which is the subject of an extensive study by Mark Slobin (2000), is a scene that has developed over the past thirty-five or so years, using older klezmer repertoire as a point of departure for creative explorations. Klezmer revival groups usually play klezmer because they like it. Most musicians in these groups discovered klezmer well into their musical careers and find that it provides them with both a creative outlet and a new means of income. Jack Kessler, a transplanted cantor from Boston, founded the Goldene Medina Klezmer Band in 1987 and currently leads the Klingon Klezmer Band. He is quick to articulate the difference between his band and others on the Philly scene:

> Put it this way, we're not a G. B. band, okay? And all the other guys are. Even the other band that call themselves specialists in Jewish weddings are basically G. B. bands.[11] (Kessler 1998)

Kessler draws his repertoire from many sources including Philadelphia's old-time repertoire, but has never been aware of any special resonance with that repertoire among local clientele:

> As for the perception of the Jewish wedding band clients, nobody knows from borsht. I inherited a book of stuff from Harold Karabell [an older generation clarinetist who worked with him briefly before his untimely death in the mid-1990s]. We have less than ten of those tunes in our regular book. Some of the older folks who actually lived that back then probably would recognize some of that stuff, but they are very much in the minority. (Kessler 1998)

Kessler constructs his parties much like a contemporary disk jockey would construct a radio show:

> The way I program my sets is for variety. There's any number of klez tunes, especially when you get into the bulgars, where one sounds like another . . .

The challenge in having a really good working repertoire for a klez band is getting enough musical variety in your envelope. (Kessler 1998)

Jewish identity is also a factor that means something to Kessler:

It is an all-Jewish band, and, not that the guys themselves are necessarily heavily into observance, but I think all of them would agree that there is a special vibe about the band. What we do is way different from what anybody else does, in terms of the Jewish content. And, besides that, we've got ambitions. We're not trying to re-create any kind of purist turn-of-the century Yiddish theater vibe. . . . We're really more like the Klezmatics.[12] (Kessler 1998)

The contemporary approach has worked well in Philadelphia, a city that was also the home of the annual Intergalactic Klezmer Festival, organized by maverick klezmer revivalist Ben Laden. In the spirit of the late Sun Ra, a dominant presence in Philadelphia's creative music scene for more than thirty years and an iconic philosopher of outsider identity politics, the festival expressed its "radical Jewish culture" mix using interplanetary metaphors that underscore the gulf between creative and mainstream musical expression:

The 6th Annual InterGalactic Jewish Music Festival, November 26, 2000: EARTHDATEAlpheratz,AndromedaWWW.GEOCITIES.COM /SPACEJEW6: After five years of presenting new Jewish music to audiences in Philadelphia, the InterGalactic Jewish Music Festival has gone truly InterGalactic and will hold this year's festival on the star Alpheratz in the Andromeda galaxy. Performances by these Jewish groups from different galaxies will highlight this year's festival: Warm Purple Gefilte, The Really Lost Tribe Band, Super Nova Lox, Nebulae Nebbish Noise. These earthly bands will also participate in this year's festival: The Rabbinical School Dropouts, Charming Hostess, The Klezmonauts, The Klingon Klezmer Band, Frank London's Invocations. InterGalactic premiere 11/26/00 Andromeda (Philadelphia). Earth premiere on 12/19/00 Merkin Hall NYC: Benny and the Vildachayas, Naftule's Dream. To attend this year's festival, attendees will have to book travel to Alpheratz, or participate remotely through an Internet WEB Portal. The communication portal will enable earthlings to sample music from this year's festival without traveling to Alpheratz. (Laden 2000, pers. comm.)

Indeed, Laden's intergalactic festival was galaxies away from Philadelphia's traditional klezmer scene. Yet, by the end of the twentieth century, its presence in Philadelphia was significant, showing, if nothing else, that, in its own quirky way, the city's Jewish music tradition was finally on track with the rest of the klezmer world.

II

Musical Traditions

4

Klezmer at Philadelphia's Jewish Weddings

This chapter examines the klezmer and Yiddish musical component of Philadelphia's twentieth-century Jewish wedding celebrations. Although klezmorim performed at many types of Jewish celebratory events, including bar mitzvahs, *pidyonim habanim* (rituals involving the redemption of first-born boys, thirty days after birth), *brit hamilot* or brises (ceremonies celebrating the male circumcision ritual), landsmanshaft parties, ladies auxiliary meetings, and Torah scroll dedications,[1] it was their function at the wedding that most vividly defined their role in Jewish society. For immigrant Jews (as well as other immigrant groups) weddings were a safe "new-world" outlet for uninhibited, unbridled quasi-religious ritual expression and, as such, are crucial to understanding how the klezmer's role in Eastern Europe reconstituted itself on American shores.[2] The evolution of Philadelphia's Jewish wedding music tradition mirrors the economic and social progress of that city's Jewish community as its members took their place in American society.

Weddings are pivotal events in any community that celebrates them. They are also events that mark a significant change in the life of a couple, what anthropologists call a "liminal" event.[3] In nearly every society, such events have required special rituals, dances, and music, and Philadelphia's transplanted Eastern European Jewish community was certainly no exception. Consequently, a musical repertoire that had little to do with the everyday experience of Jewish Americans regularly came to life at such events—and, to some extent, still does.

A wedding is also an event where rituals and traditions carry different levels of meaning for different generations. For an immigrant father of the bride, the bulgar may be his own (Bessarabian Jewish co-territorial) dance; for his daughter it is her father's dance (which she may or may not want to participate in); for her son it can be a lively reminder of family roots; and for those outside the family the dance can have a myriad of other simultaneous meanings. Looking at it from another perspective, in the early years of immigration the dance was part of an imported European tradition; for the next generation it becomes part of the "Philadelphia" tradition; later on it might be abandoned as "corny and archaic" (Rothman 1998); and finally it might come back as a "hip" component of a revival. To appreciate the progression of wedding music customs in Philadelphia, I divide this chapter's examination of Jewish wedding music into three eras: late nineteenth-century Europe, the immigrant period (pre-1924), and the age of the "standard" wedding (mid-1920s to early 1950s).

A European Wedding

European wedding customs varied according to region and the specific religious orientation of the wedding party, but in every event the music of the klezmer was deeply intertwined with each moment of the Jewish celebration. This is why Jewish folklore attributed such importance to the klezmer's contribution.[4] At traditional Jewish weddings, the klezmer's involvement might begin with the welcoming of the groom and his parents on their arrival (whenever that might be) from another city or town, or it could start with the bride's procession to the *mikve* (ritual bathhouse) the night before the wedding.[5]

A morning party would begin with a dobriden (good morning tune). Soon thereafter, there might be a kale bazetsn (bride seating) and kale baveynen (bride crying)—melancholy rubato tunes accompanying the badkhn's singing to the bride. Klezmorim accompanied the procession before the ceremony and often played a mazel-tov (congratulatory song) immediately afterward (although in some areas, mazel-tovs were women's dances played after the badekns, the veiling of the bride before the ceremony). While the wedding party ate, klezmorim played tish-nigunim (table songs), familiar melodies that were meant for listening only. The mitzve tants or kosher tants (observance dance), which sometimes followed the wedding meal, symbolized the religious commitment of the bride. It began as a social dance in the 1600s (with the women dancing with the bride and the men with the groom), but later evolved into a ritual where male or female individuals danced with the bride with a wrapped hand or handkerchief, alluding to the couple's intended future adherence to laws pertaining to family purity (Friedhaber 1985–1986: 67–68). A pantomime dance done by the older women while the bride and groom were seated was known as the challah (bread) dance; it may have been the predecessor of the contemporary *Ketsed m'radkim* (Parade Merrily), a varied and often wildly taunting pantomime. If members of the wedding party had a score to settle, they might have requested a broyges tants (anger dance), a dance in which a mock fight is followed by gestures of reconciliation. In the Hasidic milieu, this dance has evolved into the *t'khiyes hameysim* (revival of the dead) ritual, in which one participant dies in the squabble, only to be revived through the administration of a stiff drink.

By the late nineteenth century, bulgars (Romanian dances) and shers (scissors dances) were important wedding staples that included relatively complicated figures for sets of couples. Hongas and sirbas (other Romanian staples) were popular line dances, while freylekhs (happy dances) gave the entire community a chance to express their joy by dancing together in a circle.

A "stick dance" was like a game of musical chairs: Everyone walked around the chairs to the music except for the person holding the stick, who ambled about slowly, suddenly putting the stick on the floor and finding a seat. Then everyone scrambled for a seat, and the person left without one picked up the stick and the dance would start over.

If the bride was the youngest daughter and the family resided in the Ukraine or nearby, the musicians might play a mezinke tants, in which her mother would be crowned and congratulated.[6] At the end of the wedding the band would play a tearful dobrinotsh (good night tune), which would usually be followed with yet another lively freylekhs.

If the wedding were held in a large town, klezmorim would be present for the entire seven days of festivities; at those held in small shtetls where the klezmorim had to be brought in, they would usually leave after the first day. In multiple-day celebrations, the wedding party would move from house to house, and in many cases, klezmorim would provide transition music, leading the guests through the streets to the homes of various relatives playing gas nigunim (street melodies).

Philadelphia's Traditional Jewish Weddings, Pre-1930

In the first few decades after the Eastern European immigrants' arrival in the United States, celebrations reflected their new status as American Jews. In Europe, nationality was deeply intertwined with ethnic identity; in the United States, nationality became an outgrowth of shared ideological principles (democracy, liberty, and equality), and expression of ethnic identity became a matter of choice. In European homelands, competing ethnic groups often asserted their dominance through government- or church-sanctioned persecution; in the new world, freedom from persecution was theoretically not out of reach and could be secured through full participation in civic life (Hertzberg 1989: 255). Nowhere was this truer than in Philadelphia, where a thoroughly integrated ethnic ghetto (the original Port Richmond neighborhood or later South Philadelphia or the northern Liberties immigrant community) assured close contact between every type of immigrant group, and coexistence between them was remarkably peaceful. Jews took advantage of these new circumstances to integrate themselves into the relatively open and democratic society without surrendering their own distinctive ethnic characteristics.

Consequently, a wedding put together by an early twentieth-century Jewish immigrant family was, at the same time, a wedding in Philadelphia and a celebration that re-created the world of the remembered homeland. It was a time to cry on hearing the badkhn's rhymes, and dance all night *azoy vi men tantst in ades* (the way they dance in Odessa) or wherever the family came from. Charlotte Kimball Patten, a non-Jewish social worker observing Russian Jewish life in Philadelphia at the turn of the twentieth century, noted the following:

> The guests dance till four o'clock—strange old-world dances to tuneless music;[7] peasant dances from Romania, Austria and Russia; competitive dances between men, circling dances of women whirling, laughing and embracing each other.[8] It is greatly enjoyed by all except the bride, who is often desperately tired and ill after her twenty-four hours' fast. But etiquette demands that she remain until the fun is abandoned, and she bravely keeps at her post. She goes at length to her new home and another day finds her going to market while her husband is at work again in the old place in shop or factory. (Patten 1905: 245)

The character of Philadelphia's Jewish immigrant weddings was in many ways a mixture of sacred and secular, a religious ceremony followed by a wildly frivolous party. Patten astutely observed the tension between these two components at Philadelphia's Jewish weddings and social balls:

> There is among the Jews themselves no indecorum, no ever-present conscious principle of evil in the fun, which is but a coarser expression of the buffoonery that sometimes animates the New England husking bee. Judaism and Puritanism both are faithful watchdogs. But it is a certainty that the principle of evil is just at the door. (Patten 1905: 242)

As an impartial outsider, Patten was slow to condemn the Jewish approach to partying outright. Her statements reflected her desire to accept a mythology that painted the traditional Jewish world of Eastern Europe (now expressing itself in the United States) as a monolithically religious one without the internal conflicts and tensions discussed in Chapter 1, but what she actually observed told her otherwise. In reality, eroticism—the "evil" she alluded to—was very much present, as it had been since the first appearance of the klezmer in Eastern Europe (or, as religious authorities would have it, the first Jewish interaction with secular music), manifesting itself more than ever in the United States as a primary force for rebellion in what might otherwise appear to be a "puritanical rabbinically governed world" (Biale 1992: 223).[9]

The wedding was a place where dreams hatched in poverty could be turned into a fleeting reality. Jews who had little to eat in Europe made up for lost time by gorging themselves at every family gathering, eventually creating the well-known "caterer's culture." Overeating was the revenge, the apotheosis of the poor, a tangible way of proving that "the world was now different"[10] (Hertzberg 1989: 214). Fulfilling the illusion of American prosperity, a myth that continues to play itself out over and over again at Jewish weddings, already led to spending beyond the family's means at the beginning of the twentieth century, as we read in this account of an early hall wedding in Philadelphia:

> The bride and groom . . . often spend literally their last cent upon their entertainment. Yet it is cheerfully offered as a sacrifice to fate and enjoyed as an augury of future prosperity. Not long ago at the wedding of a daughter of a family desperately poor, the various sources of supply were drained to the bottom. The newly-made husband and wife were bankrupt, but every guest was fed with chicken, potatoes, bread, fruit and cake, nor were the beer and whiskey allowed to ebb. The pair was radiant and yet—tomorrow loomed from the wreckage on the tables. (Patten 1905: 244)

Early immigrant weddings were public affairs, continuing another old European tradition:

> None is denied admission. Neither the work-grimed boy, who, seeking what he may devour, drops in on his way home from his daily grind, is questioned, nor the society stranger who wears a celluloid, perhaps a linen collar, and also frankly exploits the occasion. (Patten 1905: 243)

Indeed, the casual attitude toward the booking of musicians might be seen as parallel to the casual attitude toward the timing of the affair:

> The Hall wedding invitation announces that the wedding ceremony will take place at six. An hour later, carriages call for the nearest friends of the pair and then proceed to the groom's home. Thence in procession they go for the bride and escort her to the ball. There, in front of a stage upon a raised platform painted with the immemorial sacred insignia of the Hebrew faith and punctuated with red, white and blue electric lights, the pair receive their friends. Women cry, men kiss each other and the bridal couple wait, restive until the hall is full, frightened when it is, since this is an indication that the ceremony will soon take place. When the last stragglers presumably have arrived, between ten and eleven o'clock, a large platform surmounted by the *khupe* [wedding canopy] is pushed into the middle of the floor. Willing hands are laid upon it, for whoever pushes is "forgiven many sins."[11] (Patten 1905: 244)

While the exact repertoire and order of music played at such weddings are now obscure, there is evidence that the early repertoire was a diverse one. We can sample the variety of tunes played in the early 1920s by looking at a folio notated by Morris Hoffman's father, violinist and cornetist Joseph Hoffman (1869–1945), who retired from the music business in the mid-1920s. His book (presented to the younger Hoffman in 1927) features not only a large variety of dance and concert tunes brought over from Kriovozer, a town approximately sixty miles south of Uman (from where he emigrated in 1905) but also many tunes collected later in Philadelphia. The dances include such standard genres as the hora (for example, the gasn nign), bulgar, khusidl, freylekhs (including a freylekhs that he brought over from his mother-in-law's birthplace, Bagapolye, recorded by Kandel), sirba, vengurka (Hungarian dance), doyne (Romanian shepherd's lament), dobrizhen (good morning tune), dobrinotsh (good night tune), mazel-tov (tune of congratulation), processional, Russian (Grand) march, Cossack dance, patsh tants (hand-clapping dance), tatar tants (dance of the Tartars, also known as a kavkaz, or dance from the Caucases), concert freylekhs (happy dance, in this case played for listening) mazurka (a Czech dance), waltz, sher, polka, Greek dance, matros tants (sailor's dance, a hornpipe that found its way from the British Isles to Odessa), tzigayner tants (gypsy dances), broyges tants (dance of anger), mezinke tants (to be played in honor of the mother when the youngest daughter is married off), kamarinska (a dance of Russian origin), czardas (another dance of Hungarian origin), and many early Yiddish theater favorites. We can conclude from looking at such a list that weddings in the early twentieth century were a combination of old-country customs and American innovations.

While Philadelphia's Jews often followed traditional wedding practices in the ceremony, many of the customs and dances associated with the wedding celebration reflected the relaxed attitude toward observance noted in Chapter 2.[12] This may be why Philadelphia's klezmer music folios lack many of the religious ritual dances associated with traditional European weddings, such as the kosher tants (kosher dance) or mitsve tants (commandment dance); such dances seemed to have died out in Philadelphia by the early 1920s.[13] In fact, by 1930 or so, many of the old-world dances were considered out of date (although some were later resurrected, as a freylekhs that later came back as an Israeli Hasidic dance tune), and a new standardized Philadelphia Jewish wedding music tradition emerged.

Philadelphia's Traditional Jewish Weddings, 1930–1970

It is possible to reconstruct a much fuller picture of celebrations from the mid-1930s to the late 1960s. By this time the older klezmer generation was mostly retired and there were no practicing badkhonim, only masters of ceremonies who had synthesized a standardized "American" approach to the wedding celebration. Yet the bandleaders of this era retained many Eastern European customs, packaging them in a way that suited their second-generation clientele.[14]

Weddings usually took place late on Saturday night (at least an hour after the end of the Jewish Sabbath) or any time on Sunday.[15] When the guests arrived, the bride and groom would usually be in separate rooms.[16] The musicians proceeded directly to the bride's room, where she would be seated in a large chair with flowers all around her. The older generation of musicians might begin with a dobriden, a traditional good morning or greeting tune. For the younger generation things were not as circumscribed, although they too preferred introductory music that was fairly mellow, usually popular songs of the era played as "society ballads." After an hour or two, someone would give the band the signal for the ceremony to begin.[17] At this point the musicians' role was very much standardized in a format that seamlessly blended European and American material:

> During the ceremony, when the rabbi would make a blessing, the fiddle player would play background music—they would eat this up—they would love that. And as soon as they broke the glass, this was the sign for the music to play—"Khusn, Kale, Mazeltov." To walk down the aisle, it was "Here Comes the Bride," there was no other song.[18] And, of course, in between, the vocalist with the orchestra sang "Oh, Promise Me" or "Because." There was no such thing as a request. (Uhr 1998)

A reception line for the bride and groom and their family immediately followed the ceremony. Next came the Grand March (a custom already noted in Patten's 1905 study[19]) where the family led the other guests around the room. The most popular of these marches was the Russian military march, "Tosca po rodine" (Homesickness, Figure 4.1).

Figure 4.1. The Russian military march, "Tosca po rodine."

Caterer Bernie Uhr recalls how the Grand March functioned at his family's restaurant during his tenure:

> Before the family went downstairs to eat, they had to clear with us whether we were ready for them. If we weren't, the emcee would make what was called a "Grand March," where he would zigzag the couples,

and then separate them, and the bride and groom danced. He did it as long as we needed time. If we didn't need time, the announcement came and you went right downstairs. If we needed time, that march could take forever. (Uhr 1998)

Next, the bride and groom disappeared for a short period of intimacy[20] known as *yikhud* (eighteen minutes of isolation), and the guests proceeded into the dining room, where the band played quietly. When the bride and groom returned, it was time for the first freylekhs, a short traditional dance in honor of the bride and her family. For this dance, the band would usually play the tune known as "Pasey's Freylekhs" (Figure 4.2; for the story of this dance tune's title, see Chapter 3), and only the immediate family of the bride would dance.

Figure 4.2. "Pasey's Freylekhs."

The early part of the wedding dinner was a kind of music and dancing "no-man's-land":

That was when the pressure started between the caterer and the musicians, because the caterer had all of this hot food he had to get out and serve, but the musicians had to play because they were getting paid for it. (Borock 1997a)

During this era, most catering halls had small stages equipped with a piano and one microphone. One ubiquitous ritual at the beginning of the dinner was the introduction of the bride and groom. They remained standing as the orchestra played "The Star Spangled Banner" and "Hatikvah," Israel's national anthem. (and, before the state of Israel was established, the Anthem of the World Zionist Organization since 1897). Then the emcee read telegrams from the president or other phony greetings meant to get laughs.[21] He would also recite a standard wedding toast: "I wish you luck, I wish you joy, I wish you first a baby boy, and when his hair begins to curl, I wish you then a baby girl" (Uhr 1998).

When the waiters brought the food to the tables, it was a clear signal for the musicians to stop playing dance music and switch to background music. In the early years tish nigunim (table songs) khusidls, doynes, and concert freylekhs were most frequently used for this purpose. By the 1930s horas and tatar tantsn joined the dinner music repertoire, even after the dances that went with them faded from memory.[22] After the food was served, the musicians might leave the bandstand and stroll (or "play tables"), a lucrative source for extra tips. By the 1940s, the dinner music repertoire had changed:

> At the dinner table, we would play songs from the Jewish Theater; "In mayn oygn bistu sheyn" (In My Eyes You Are Beautiful), "Bay mir bistu sheyn" (To Me, You're Beautiful), "Mayn tayere" (My Dear One), "Sheyn vi di l'vone" (Beautiful as the Moon), or "Git mir op mayn harts tsurik" (Give Me Back My Heart). These weren't for dancing; they were for listening while the people ate, or while the waiters served the soup.[23] (Borock 1997a)

After dinner, the serious dancing started. Indeed, while the wedding technically framed everything following the ceremony as part of a *seudah* (sacred meal), by the 1930s very few Philadelphia Jewish weddings featured separate-sex seating or dancing. Moreover, hardly any of the popular Jewish wedding dances carried religious connotations; their roots were more in European folkdance— in dances such as the kasab tants (butcher's dance) or the gallop and quadrille. The heritage they evoked was not a religious one or even a Jewish one, but that of the European homeland: At a wedding a Jew could be a Cossack, a Greek butcher, or a Romanian Gypsy. Indeed, the repertoire itself also proved quite serviceable at Greek, Romanian, Ukrainian, Gypsy, Armenian, Serbian, and Russian weddings.

The bulgar was an extremely popular wedding dance among early Jewish immigrants, and by the 1940s it dominated the repertoire.[24] It had its roots in the Romanian bulgaresca and was done by couples who performed square-dance–like figures and other steps in circles. It also allowed for a practice known as "shining," in which the individual was allowed to show off his or her special steps. Philadelphia's klezmorim (and Jewish patrons) took a liking to march-like

Figure 4.3. "Bucharester Bulgar" from 1927.

Romanian-style bulgars; one of these, known in Kandel's recording as the "Bucharester Bulgar," is still played by many bands at contemporary Philadelphia weddings in a medley with the obligatory "Hava nagila" (Let's Rejoice; Block 1998). Figure 4.3 shows both Hoffman's 1927 transcription of this bulgar as it was played in the 1910s and 1920s and a transcription of a 1950s and 1960s version. This tune's longevity makes it an ideal example through which to observe the twentieth-century transformation of klezmer. Over the years, the key was changed from G minor to D minor, the harmony of the A section became the melody, and the tempo increased considerably.

Local musicians composed many popular tunes in this idiom. Trumpeter Max Petrofsky wrote staples such as "Chaikele" (in honor of his wife)[25] and "Shvartse Oygn" (Black Eyes), and bulgars composed by Harry Swerdlow and Jacob Hoffman found their way into many folios. The names of bulgars often had their own histories having nothing to do with their origin, as shown in this anecdote concerning the "Shnoz Bulgar":

Bukharester Bulgar (From Adler, 1955, Zeft, 1968)

Figure 4.3. Continued.

Jack Lewis (whose original name was Max Essner) was one of the popular leaders, and he had a drummer, named Ray Dinnenberg. His nickname was "The Shnoz," since he had a very prominent nose. So whenever we played this particular bulgar we would sing "ya, da, da, da, da, da, da, Hooray for the Shnoz!" (Hoffman 1997)

Another wedding favorite was the freylekhs, a group dance for an unlimited number of guests who held hands or placed their arms on each other's shoulders and moved in a circle. As mentioned in Chapter 1, the freylekhs had gone under a variety of names in Europe: hopke, redl (circle), karahod (round dance), dreydl (top), kaylekhiks (round), and rikudl (dance), although in Philadelphia it was always called a freylekhs. It was usually danced at a moderately brisk pace, but when there were elderly persons in the circle the tempo would be slower (Beregovski 2001).[26] Most freylekhs have two or three sections and are composed of eight- or sixteen-bar phrases. They tend to have phrases that revolve around sixteenth note figures.

A broyges tants (anger dance, Figure 4.4) would be requested by guests who wished to settle a score, ranging from the traditional mock animosity between the mother of the bride and the mother of the groom, to an overture asking for forgiveness of a large debt. This dance included thirty-two measures of stalking and threatening gestures, followed by a congenial freylekhs of indeterminate length.

Broyges tants (from Kandel, 1921)

Figure 4.4. A typical broyges tants.

Another popular request was the "Dance for the Old Men," a slow khusidl (Hasidic dance) that served as a kind of relic through the 1950s. Here the men would try to re-create the mock (or sometimes real) Hasidic dances they remembered from their own European grandparents, many of whom came from Hasidic backgrounds (Figure 4.5).

Dance (khusidl) For The Old Men, from Swerdlow, 1945

Figure 4.5. A slow khusidl (Hasidic dance) that served as a kind of relic through the 1950s.

One of the most memorable and most intricately ritualized parts of any Philadelphia Jewish wedding celebration was the krinsl (crowning) or mezinke (youngest daughter) ceremony (Figure 4.6). Indeed, these staged moments formed a uniquely American counterpart to the religious rituals of the wedding ceremony.[27] In Europe, this dance was done only when the bride was the last daughter in the family to be married, and it focused only on her mother. American bandleaders expanded it to include a large number of other family members.[28] Bandleader Bobby Block describes the krinsl (mezinke) ceremony he learned from older leaders:

> I put four chairs out in the center of the floor for the four parents, the two mothers in the center and their spouses on either side. If both mothers are being crowned (if the groom is also the youngest) we call that a double crowning, but even if only one is being crowned we seat both sets of parents out of *koved* (respect) and because this is now a brand-new family. If there are grandparents, I seat them as well.[29] Then, I get [all the guests] to form a huge circle around these chairs, around the whole perimeter of the ballroom floor, and we start to play "The Mezinke"[30] very slowly, so that everyone can clap their hands on the backbeat. I explain that this is an old Jewish custom, that on the night of her last daughter's marriage, the mother is to be crowned, as a queen is crowned. The crown is made of flowers; the flowers symbolize the sweetness of motherhood. And then we welcome all of the siblings who come out to congratulate their parents, and if there are grandchildren, they come with them, and they go up and kiss the parents and then stand behind them. After that, I introduce the bride and groom, who bring the crown with them, and when they come out we start to play it half-time, more dramatically, and they kiss their parents and stand directly behind the

two mothers. Everyone gives them all a round of applause. Then I tell everyone to join hands, and we go into "Ot azoy tantsn mitn shviger" (That's the Way We Dance with the Mother-in-Law),[31] "Sheyne kale" (Pretty Bride),[32] the "Patsh tants" (Hand-Clapping Dance),[33] and "Mekhuteyneste mayne" (My Dear Mother-in Law"). The family stays in the middle, and everyone dances around them and congratulates them. (Block 1999)[34]

Another essential wedding dance was the Russian Sher, to be discussed at length in Chapter 5.

Figure 4.6. Music commonly used in Philadelphia's krinsl ceremony.

Traditional Jewish weddings were known even outside the Jewish community for their extraordinary revelry. When assimilationist tendencies took hold, the character of the music could be a significant bone of contention between the bride and her parents, as in this anecdote:

> I remember an affair where the bride said to Danny Shankin, the leader, "I don't want any Jewish music. I want just American." And all afternoon there was no Jewish. But for some reason the photographer took the bridal

Figure 4.6. Continued.

party outside to take a picture. And somebody came over to him and said "Don't you know any Jewish?" It seemed like a gentile man. So, he says, "Yes, we do." So the man said, "Well, I want to dance in a circle, you know." So he played a Jewish number. And the bride came back in while it was on and saw all these people up dancing. So she goes over to Danny and says, "Play what you want." So when it was all over and she's paying the band Danny asks, "Why was it that you didn't want any Jewish?" So she says "Well, my boss is gentile, and I was just embarrassed. . . . But for six months before the wedding everyone was telling him how he was gonna dance in circles, and he never told me." (Uhr 1998)

By the 1920s, Philadelphia's Jewish weddings almost always included sets of American background and dance music. One of Philadelphia's most idiosyncratic customs was the mummer's strut, usually performed to the popular minstrel-era reel, "Oh, Dem Golden Slippers." Polkas, waltzes, and mazurkas persisted, taking their place next to vaudeville hits from the 1920s and to current show tunes and Yiddish theater hits in dance arrangements, such as "Sheyn vi di l'vone" (Lovely as the Moon).

Even if the wedding repertoire consisted of mixed American and Jewish music, the band usually played all Jewish repertoire for the final hour. At the designated ending time the musicians would sign off with a dobrinotsh or gute nakht ("Good Night Waltz"), a very slow and sentimental tune. Philadelphia had its own gute nakht, known commonly to Ukranian klezmorim as "Platsh yisroel" (Cry, Israel, Figure 4.7).[35] The tune also had great longevity in the Ukraine

Figure 4.7. "Good Night Waltz," Platsh yisroel.

and was among those officially banned when Soviet authorities attempted to silence Jewish music in the 1960s.

Weddings arranged through union bandleaders were always contracted for a specific time period, but it was not unusual for them to go much longer. When it came to paying overtime (the practice of compensating musicians for additional hours), the old European customs prevailed:

> The musicians could agree that it was a three-hour affair or a four-hour affair, but they never really knew when it would be over. It wasn't unusual for them to stay until one or two in the morning without a price [after the agreed-upon sum had been exceeded] because they were getting [tips] from the uncle from New York, or the sister's husband, and they used to put it in the fiddle case, since the leader was usually a fiddle player. When they took their ties off, they divided what was in the kitty. I even remember orchestras going back to the house, or playing in the street, because they knew there was a five dollar bill or a ten-dollar bill involved, so they went. (Uhr 1998)

From the musicians' perspective, such affairs were simply business as usual:

> When we played for live-wire affairs, we'd play till three, four o'clock in the morning. . . . Let's say the man who ran the affair was short of funds, they'd pass the hat around, make a collection, pay the money up, (and say) "Play another hour!" Sometimes we'd play till four or five o'clock. Now when I'd play for the Kriovozer crowd, they went to town. After the dinner they got started, I'd come home and see the milkman (delivering the) milk. (Hoffman 1997a)

> Those weddings went on all night. . . . In the old days they'd leave the hall and the band would go with them and parade through the streets to one of the homes (of the relatives). There was one occasion where the bride and groom were getting a plane to go away on their honeymoon, and the whole band got into cabs, went out to the airport, and they played up to the airplane, the trumpet player was there, the saxophone player was there, the trombone player came, and we danced Jewish right there on the runway. It was partying—we liked to party. (Borock and Netsky 1999)

By the late 1940s, "traditional" Jewish bandleaders found themselves engaged in strict competition with society-style leaders who marketed their own party packages for the bride's generation. These society-style leaders, who followed an American corporate business model, created a new kind of Jewish wedding (see Chapter 3). Still, it is interesting to note how long many late nineteenth-century wedding customs lasted in Philadelphia: Ceremonies noted by Patten in 1905 were still observed at some weddings chronicled as late as 1970. Corny and archaic as these customs may have seemed to the younger generation, the slow build and ritualized fun of the "standard" Philadelphia Jewish wedding had a curve to it that made for a good (and long) party, albeit a party that could not last forever in America.

5

The Evolution of Philadelphia's
Russian Sher Medley

"There was a marvelous famous sher. That was a big deal."

—David Raksin (1998), Hollywood film composer
and former Philadelphia klezmer

This chapter traces the history of the Philadelphia Russian Sher medley, the musicians who created it, and the community that reveled to it in their celebrations, from the late nineteenth century to the present. While many other dance tunes, including bulgars, freylekhs, horas, a mezinke medley celebrating the marriage of the youngest daughter, and a dobrinotsh, a good night waltz, were also unique to the Philadelphia klezmer repertoire (see Chapter 4), a particular sher medley became closely identified with this city, even by musicians from elsewhere.[1] This transplanted European klezmer dance medley became known as the "Philadelphia Sher," the "Philadelphia Sherele," or the "Philadelphia Russian Sher."

The dance known in Yiddish as the sher derives its name from the German *Schere* (scissors). In English the dance was usually called the Russian Sher. It rose to its position of prominence in the nineteenth century and remained an indispensable feature of Philadelphia's Jewish weddings through the 1950s. As mentioned in previous chapters, during the period of mass immigration, American Jewish weddings indexed the community's relationship to its European past, and the music played at these weddings—the Russian Sher in particular—was a sensitive barometer of that relationship. In the 1960s, the dance was seldom played at weddings, but lived on at gatherings held by Jewish fraternal organizations.

The decline and eventual disappearance of the music and the dance associated with the sher coincided with a move away from the Yiddish language and toward a self-conscious embrace of American values and styles. Thus, like so many Eastern European aspects of American Jewish culture, the evolution of the sher follows a seemingly inevitable path in the direction of entropy as the dance lost its status as an integral part of a Jewish party and then reemerged as a nostalgic commemoration of an older form of expression. Not surprisingly, it has become a cornerstone in the recent revival of what has come to be known as klezmer music and of the Eastern European Jewish dances associated with that music.

Thanks to a uniquely complete body of evidence, including manuscripts and recordings, as well as interviews with old-time musicians, it is possible to trace the processes through which small instrumental groupings gave way to larger ones (and later to smaller regroupings), codified versions of the medley emerged, older European-style sections became interspersed with more contemporary material, meticulous transcriptions were abandoned in favor of half-remembered fragments, and a gradual decline in interest led to the dance's disappearance and the medley's obsolescence. The history of Philadelphia's Russian Sher paints a vivid sonic portrait of an American Jewish community as reflected in the shifting social relations and ways of making music over a period of more than five decades.[2]

The European Legacy

A set dance for four couples that takes fifteen to twenty minutes to complete, the Russian Sher is related to other popular Euro-American social dances, including American square and contra dances and, most notably, the quadrille, a dance of French origin that is found in many variants around the world.[3] The sher is in the tradition of courtship dances that have their roots in Provencal court dance at the time of the Crusades; these dances embodied a polite code of social behavior in contrast with older dances in which men would pick women up and carry them into a circle. The new code of social behavior substituted less overtly physical expressions of dominance; for example, the bowing or turning that can be seen in the sher (Lawson 1953).

While little is known about the early history of the sher, a *Scherer Oder Schartanz* (scissors or crowd dance) dating from 1562 is found in Bohme's *Collection of German Dances*. This 2/4 dance has a phrase structure similar to the popular Jewish version, and pioneering Jewish ethnomusicologist Moshe Beregovski hypothesizes that Ashkenazi Jews adapted their sher medleys from the (now obscure) German ones, eventually employing characteristic Jewish dance steps and "easternized" melodies more typical of Eastern Europe, where most Jews lived during the nineteenth-century. One of several popular couple dances originally performed by Jewish women, the sher was part of a long-standing strenuously athletic tradition of same-sex Jewish dancing,[4] although, in the twentieth century, it functioned primarily as a mixed couple dance.

The most flamboyant and individualistic moves in the sher, as in other East European Jewish dances, were characterized as "shining," a combination of dramatic arm gestures, head tilts, and strutting that gave the dance a strong Eastern European flavor. Particular communities later introduced their own steps and gestures to the sher. In Cuba, for example, dancers would rotate their hips in a way reminiscent of Latin dancing (Kagansky 2000).[5] The sher's demise in the

United States has been linked to the advent of American and Latin-style mixed ballroom and Israeli dancing at American Jewish celebrations.

Dancing the Sher in Twentieth-Century Philadelphia

At Philadelphia's Jewish celebrations, the sher was not a standard part of the repertoire, but rather was a "request number." The person who requested the sher was obligated to pay the musicians a substantial tip. The bandleader would then dedicate the number to the patron, who would invite others to join him or her in the dance and serve as the "leader" once it started. In the 1920s and 1930s, shers were usually played for only one set of eight dancers at a time. This made it a lucrative dance for the musicians because, over the course of an evening, several different guests or groups of guests would put together sets of their own and commission a sher performance exclusively for their own dancing. In the 1940s the sher became more of a communal dance, with a large number of wedding guests taking to the floor at one time. In either case, Bernie Uhr (born 1923), manager of several of Philadelphia's most popular catering institutions and an excellent dancer in his own right, recalled that "the musicians would play a sher till everybody dropped." He also remembered how Philadelphia musicians let the crowd know that the dance was soon to begin: "The musicians played a signal, and then they stopped till everybody got together into [sets], and then the dance started" (Uhr 1998).[6] The "signal" consisted of the first eight measures of the opening phrase of sher #1, culminating in an abrupt ending, as the musicians waited for the dancers to get ready. Clarinetist Joe Borock recalls that all the guests knew the protocol and were ready to contribute funds when the time came:

> When you went to a wedding you had to have at least three dollars in your pocket. The first dollar was for the coat-check girl who was usually the daughter of the caterer—if you didn't have a dollar you wouldn't get your clothes back. Number two was for the fiddle-player when he went around to the tables, and the third was for the sher. If the guests didn't have the money for a sher you just sat with your arms folded. (Borock 1997a)

The Structure of the Dance

The dance steps associated with Philadelphia's Russian Sher medley are similar to those used in shers danced by recent Jewish immigrants from the southern Ukraine. The dance consists of four figures:

> Figure 1: "Circle." Couples (with man on left, woman on right) circle right for sixteen counts, then turn around and circle left for sixteen counts, usually ending the figure with a "one, two, three." This figure is often done twice.

Figure 2: "Promenade." Couples promenade in a circle with the woman on the outside for sixteen counts, usually ending with the man turning the woman.

Figure 3: "Crossing." Couples one and three take four steps forward, then four steps back, and then eight steps across, usually passing on the right and turning on the last two counts. Then couples two and four do the same.

Figure 4: "Leading Out" (*aroysfirn*). The "number one" man "sets up" (gets in position) for eight beats, dances with his partner for eight beats, sets up again for eight beats, dances with his corner (*shokhn*) for eight beats, sets up again, dances with his partner again, and then dances with each of the other women in the circle, continuing the pattern. The tradition of "checking in with one's partner" after dancing with all of the other women in the set made the Philadelphia version of the sher unusually long. It was during this part of the dance that the practice of shining (mentioned earlier) was especially encouraged.

In all versions of the sher, after the four figures were completed, the entire dance would be repeated three more times. Each man would dance with each of the women following the same formula just mapped out. If more than one set was on the dance floor after everyone completed all of the figures, all of the participating couples would form a long line and smoothly promenade around the room.[7] On completion of the promenade, they would join hands and "thread the needle." This part of the dance required the leader to form a chain and lead the front of the line under the arms of dancers in the middle, a pattern that was repeated several times, until everyone was eventually led into a tangled mass. Then, the leader would retrace his or her steps, and the chain would slowly unravel.[8] This last part of the dance required participants to become more intimately intertwined than some guests cared to be, and by this point in the dance, shers sometimes degenerated into fights. Indeed, according to musician Joe Borock, fighting was so common that, in his long career, he had never seen a sher reach its conclusion (Borock 1997b).[9]

Although the choreographed dance figures that comprise the sher are invariably eight measures in length, they do not always correlate directly with eight-bar musical phrases. Eastern European Jewish dance revivalist Michael Alpert makes this point in these instructions to a group of New York–based dancers:

Ideally, [the sher] should have a sense of constant motion, like the gears of a clock, with people always turning. If you're not the one dancing in the middle [you] dance in place. Traditionally, when people do it, the steps are not in sync with the musical phrase; nobody cares about the musical phrase—what's important is the rhythm. . . . so that you may do a figure and it takes longer than a phrase it overlaps, it's a little disconcerting in a certain way. But what's important is the rhythm, and what's important is that you keep dancing.[10] (Alpert 1988, home video)

While the music used for some sher medleys (including those popular among New York musicians) is often composed exclusively of eight-, sixteen-, and thirty-two–measure phrases, a variety of phrase lengths appear in other examples. The typical Philadelphia Sher medley includes at least eight twelve-bar phrases (each repeated so as to create twenty-four–bar sections). These longer phrases may represent an attempt by the musicians to provide "signal" phrases that allow the couples enough time to get into position, while also generating clear cues to help the musicians and dancers coordinate the phrasing of the dance steps, even if only approximately, with the phrasing of the music.

Philadelphia's Russian Sher Medley

As was already noted, the music traditionally played for the sher was usually sequenced in long medleys that may or may not have been determined before the dance began. Ethnomusicologist Walter Zev Feldman (2002: 113) categorizes the traditional music played for sher medleys as "core" (or uniquely Jewish) klezmer repertoire. The musical material found in all of these dances is in 2/4 meter and derives entirely from duple subdivisions; there are no triplets, as there would be in the Romanian sirba or bulgar. As I mentioned earlier, other lively traditionally Jewish 2/4 dances include the skotshne and the freylekhs. Tunes used for a sher medley are, in fact, often recycled freylekhs; a tune played for a sher in one town might be played for a freylekhs in another. Indeed, as Beregovski points out in his study of the European klezmer tradition, once a specific musician established a tune as part of a sher medley, that tune would no longer be played in a section of a freylekhs. In this way, particular sher medleys often came to be associated with specific geographical points of origin. Interestingly, this tradition continued in the United States, with distinctive sher medleys taking root in Milwaukee, New York, and Philadelphia, among other places. Where there was no ancestral klezmer tradition to draw on or where those traditions were put aside, musicians turned to the New York Russian Sher, which was published in the early 1920s in the Kammen Bros. popular Jewish wedding music folio. For this reason, the opening sections of the New York Russian Sher medley became the standard in many parts of the country and even around the world.

While klezmer research has generally suffered from a lack of documentation (see Slobin 2000: 93), the music played for the Philadelphia Russian Sher medley is exceptionally well documented. I was fortunate to find eleven complete versions, including eight manuscripts and two recorded renditions, in addition to several partial recordings and manuscripts and one published excerpt from the nineteenth century. These manuscripts, recordings, interviews, and observations were made available to me by active and retired musicians from klezmer backgrounds, children and grandchildren of klezmer musicians, and my own relatives. Taken together, they form a series of snapshots from different eras that reveal, in unprecedented detail, not only a history of the Philadelphia Russian Sher medley in the twentieth century but also clues to the history and cultural sensibilities of the community that played it and danced to it.

What are the distinctive features of the Philadelphia Russian Sher medley? It was exceptionally long, consistent, and stable. The music was usually sequenced in seventeen- to twenty-minute medleys, with fixed key (tonic) relationships, a practice that remained consistent through the 1960s. The effort that Philadelphia's musicians made to adhere to such a consistent structure in these medleys over such a long period of time contrasted with what we know about the practice of musicians in other American cities. Elsewhere, by the 1940s, sher medleys generally consisted of two or three set sections, after which the musicians added popular folk, theater, and dance tunes drawn from their common repertoire. As Feldman (2002: 115–116) notes in his study of the bulgar, by the mid-twentieth century, American musicians had ceased to distinguish between various types of lively wedding dances and were incorporating sirbas and bulgars, as well as the more traditional freylekhs, into their sher medleys.[11] By the late 1960s, a less rigorous approach had also taken hold among some Philadelphia musicians, so much so that knowledge of the entire sher medley from start to finish became a barometer both of one's technical skill as a musician and of one's serious commitment to the klezmer scene. If you either did not know the sher or could not make it though the sher, you were, quite plainly, not fit to share the stage with those who did or could.

The stability of the Philadelphia Russian Sher medley reflected the emphasis of Philadelphia's musicians on knowing, memorizing, and retaining the components of the sher, a feat that represented a high level of accomplishment. It was essential that someone, if not the entire band, know the sher by memory because, as can be seen in Harry Swerdlow's popular hand-notated klezmer folios from the 1940s, the entire piece took up eight full pages of music, with virtually all of the page turns in the middle of musical phrases. There was no one to turn the pages for the musicians, and at least one member of the band had to be able to lead the others through the piece with no hesitation. In my research, it quickly became obvious who such players were. They needed nothing more than several measures of the opening phrase to launch into an entire eight-page medley by heart. Thus, Berl Freedman—a classically trained violinist from Buki (near Kiev in the Ukraine) who served as both contractor and copyist for the orchestra of the Arch Street Yiddish Theatre and for Harry Kandel's Victor recording orchestra—only notated the first few measures of the Philadelphia Russian Sher medley, whereas he wrote out other pieces in their entirety (Figure 5.1).

Fortunately, for the sake of posterity, others were less casual about committing their sher medleys to paper. In fact, by the late 1920s, as more and more musicians from outside the traditional klezmer orbit entered the Jewish wedding music scene, complete manuscript versions of tunes and medleys became quite common. Music-store owner Morris Freed published a nine-page sheet music edition of the Philadelphia Russian Sher medley as he knew it in 1914,

Figure 5.1. Berl Freedman's Philadelphia Russian Sher medley manuscript.

while others proudly wrote out their sprawling versions for students and clients. Clarinetist Jerry Adler somehow managed to crowd most of his manuscript onto two very densely packed pages, and cornetist Joseph Hoffman fit his on three pages. Still, despite the existence of printed sources, the form of Philadelphia's Russian Sher medley evolved through a gradual process of accretion, deletion, and innovation, the same process that has been documented for English folk ballads and Irish reels. For example, reconstructing the genealogy of "O'Dowd's #9I," Ciaran Carson (1997: 90) writes,

> The tune becomes a family tree. It is a conversation piece, a modus operandi, a way of renegotiating lost time. Our knowledge of the past is changed each time we hear it; our present time, imbued with yesterday, comes out with bent dimensions. Slipping in and out of nodes of time, we find our circles sometimes intersect with others. Yet there is a wider circle we can only dimly comprehend, whose congregation is uncountable, whose brains and hands have shaped this tune in ways unknowable to us. We do not know how far or deep its palimpsests extend.

In the case of Philadelphia's Russian Sher medley, some of the actual manuscripts are literally palimpsests, with traces of earlier markings vaguely visible through the most recently pasted revisions.

One can also, of course, attribute a fair amount of fluidity to the imaginations of the musicians themselves, who played with each other in various constellations and across generations, forming interconnecting circles of musical performance, transmission, and repertoire. Since there were various versions of the sher that leaders might call up without notice, a sideman had to have lots of sections at his fingertips. Trumpeter Marvin Katz describes the process as he remembers it in the early 1950s:

> It all depended on whom you were playing with; the order wasn't always the same and some of the leaders didn't know all of the sections . . . . If you were playing with Jerry Adler it was one thing, with Lou Orkin it was another, with Joe Borock it was quite a different thing. If I played with Ray Sheinfeld I would lead it myself. The most important thing was to know all of the sections so that nothing would surprise you. That Swerdlow book you gave me actually had all of the sections,[12] but I didn't have one of those back then. (M. Katz 2002)

There were indeed a lot of sections for a 1950s musician to know, as there had been in the 1920s and 1930s and, undoubtedly, earlier as well. Beregovski (2011: 11) points out that, in Eastern Europe, every kapelye had several established tunes it played for the sher.

Not surprisingly, Philadelphia's older klezmer folios contain remnants of earlier shers that musicians brought over from Europe. In Harry Kandel's hand-notated wedding folio, dating from before 1915,[13] the following obscure melody appears as sher #4, but is not heard on either of Kandel's sher recordings, nor does it appear in any of the other ten renditions in my possession (Figure 5.2). A 1920s folio from the Freedman family contains the well-known "Berditchever Sher," attributed to the Hasidic rebbe Levi Yitzkhak of Berditchev (Figure 5.3).

Kandel, Sher #4, ca. 1910

Figure 5.2. Kandel Folio Sher #4.

Figure 5.3. "Berditchever Sher."

In Wolff Kostakowsky's 1916 *Hebrew Wedding Music Folio*, we find this lovely European-style tune as part of the "Philadelphia Sherele" (Figure 5.4); this was recorded by Khevrisa, a groundbreaking and influential traditionalist klezmer ensemble.

These tunes are indicative of the diverse material that made up the earliest sher medleys played in Philadelphia. By the second decade of the twentieth

Figure 5.4. "Philadelphia Sherele."

century they were being abandoned in Philadelphia, while other tunes were entering the mix that would become what we now think of as the Philadelphia Russian Sher medley.

A Short History of Philadelphia's Russian Sher Medley

Despite Philadelphia's long retention of the sher medley (in much of its classic complexity), the piece did evolve over time, reflecting changes that took place within Philadelphia's Jewish community. In 1915, for instance, we see a piece that reflects a community's shared immigrant origins; in the 1930s we find a medley that mirrors the aesthetics of a second generation of musicians, at home in Philadelphia and determined to reconstruct their musical repertoire in a way more consonant with the tastes of their audience. In the 1940s, we encounter a community and a sher medley with a more cosmopolitan outlook, and in the 1960s we find a community that has relatively little use for an old-world dance.

Through all of these changes, the piece remains very much a local phenomenon, a Philadelphia mix that reflects the tastes of that city's close-knit Jewish community and collection of musicians. Its unique tunes create a soundscape that belongs in Philadelphia's catering halls and is compatible with certain foods prepared in a particular way. As the legacy of local musicians and their families, it is just the right music for this place, compatible with all of the idiosyncrasies of local Jewish tastes: egg bagels, Levis's hot dogs, Shupak's sour pickles, Kaplan's rye bread. It is yet another banner of a proud homogeneous community that begrudgingly acknowledges the outside world while taking care to keep it at bay. The Philadelphia Russian Sher medley holds onto its unabashedly provincial character by flaunting both its conservatism and uniqueness at every turn.

The history of Philadelphia's Russian Sher medley is a microcosm of the history of Philadelphia's klezmer music tradition. The processes that shape a musical form are all but hidden from view, whether because they are embodied and rarely verbalized or because they are shrouded in professional secrecy. As mentioned in Chapters 1 and 2, Philadelphia's Jewish musicians and their Eastern European klezmer counterparts had their own esoteric occupational culture, complete with insider language and outsider reputations. Nonetheless, it is possible, through a detailed analysis of the musical evidence, broadly conceived, to reveal historical and social processes that shape and are shaped by a musical form. In the case of the Philadelphia Russian Sher medley, particular individuals with leadership or entrepreneurial talents played important roles in these processes, beginning in the late nineteenth century when the Lemisch family arrived in Philadelphia, bringing with them the shers they had played in Jassi or, in Yiddish, Yass (Romania). By the early 1880s Selig Itzik Lemisch (1819–1891) and his family had become celebrated party and theater musicians, and at least one of their shers became a cornerstone of all Philadelphia Russian Sher medleys that followed.[14] A 1914 hand-copied manuscript of violinist, cornetist, bandleader, teacher, and family patriarch Meyer Swerdlow, a practical man who wrote tunes out for students who later played in his band, represents an actual bandstand edition of his day, with an early bow to the New York Russian Sher medley—sixteen bars of it are included at the very end. Looking at such a manuscript and comparing it with medleys played elsewhere at the time, we can observe that a Philadelphia Russian Sher medley, a compilation of material brought over from Europe or crafted locally, had taken shape, with tunes and a form and structure that were unique to musicians of that city.

Critical to an understanding of the transmission and canonization of a Philadelphia Russian Sher medley was the shift from old-world European methods (oral transmission, by ear and example) to handwritten manuscripts, to printed sheet music, and finally to recordings. Thus an account of the history of the Philadelphia Russian Sher medley would need to attend to the impact of Morris Freed's 1914 sheet music edition, which made a version of the medley available for mass dissemination not only in Philadelphia but also in New York. Freed, an amateur composer, music entrepreneur, and later chess champion of the state of Pennsylvania (!), sold copies of his edition at his popular music store, which was located at Fifth and Morris Streets in the center of South Philadelphia's Jewish community, while his old-world father, Meyer, a badkhn from Belarus, repaired stringed instruments and bows in the back room. Freed's published sheet music edition served as the model for a 1920 recording by New York's Abe Schwartz Orchestra and for a long time as a handy (but outdated) text for musicians who wanted to learn the sher.

While creating the illusion of a definitive and permanent musical form, such sheet music could not, in itself, forestall shifts in popular tastes during the 1920s and 1930s. The performance of Americanized Jewish music on Jewish radio shows and in the Yiddish theater or heard on the recordings of such icons as clarinetist Dave Tarras was partly responsible for these shifts in tastes. A close examination of the musical evidence reveals how some, but not all, elements in the Freed manuscript were supplanted by a more modular construction that strung together much shorter and catchier tunes. Once these changes were consolidated, Harry or Jacob Swerdlow (two sons of Meyer Swerdlow, mentioned earlier), for a small price, wrote out a new version of the sher medley for the 1940s and 1950s generation, so that, until recently, it sat in club-date wedding music folios, gathering dust and waiting for this collector to find it. Yet, by the 1960s (as we can hear in a recorded rendition from 1968) the musicians seemed to pay very little attention to manuscripts. Instead, they incorporated other popular Jewish melodies that they learned by ear and knew by heart. Oral tradition had returned.

Musical Analysis of the Philadelphia Russian Sher Medley

Given its heterogeneous musical elements and structural flexibility, how did the Philadelphia Russian Sher manage to retain its musical identity over time?

To answer this question, I now proceed to an extended analysis of the historical development of the medley, in which I draw on the following corpus:

- Clarinetist Harry Kandel's handwritten folio (circa 1910–1915)
- Morris Freed's 1914 published edition (supplemented by an Abe Schwartz Orchestra recording from 1920)
- A 1914 handwritten folio from cornetist-violinist Meyer Swerdlow
- Wolff Kostakowsky's 1916 *Hebrew Wedding Music Folio* (published in New York)
- Harry Kandel's 1918 Victor recordings
- A 1927 manuscript version by cornetist Joseph Hoffman
- A 1940s manuscripts from clarinetist Jerry Adler
- A 1945 folio from pianist/drummer Harry Swerdlow
- A 1950s manuscript from clarinetist Lou Orkin
- The "official" Jewish dance folio of the popular Music Associates, the Jewish society music agency circa 1960 (compiled by trumpeter Norman Yablonsky and hand-copied by Al Boss, a prolific local copyist)
- A recorded rendition featuring clarinetist Jerry Adler and trumpeter Morris Zeft dating from 1968

In the following analysis I first delineate the compositional character of the Philadelphia Russian Sher medley in terms of number and sequence of sections.[15] I then characterize the tonality of the corpus to better understand the harmonic and tonal sequence it follows. Finally, I present a detailed analysis of the structure of the Philadelphia Russian Sher medley to show what changed, what stayed the same, and why the music took the form that it did in relation to the historical context in which it was played.

Composition

Although conspicuously missing from the radar screens of those who have surveyed Jewish musical composition, the Philadelphia Russian Sher medley is an imposing piece of music in its own right. Even considering the variety within it, an internal musical logic ties the parts together in ways that unify the overall structure of the composition.

Flexibility in combining units allows the musicians to vary the length of the piece in response to the contingencies of each performance situation. While the nature, number, and sequence of sections vary within each notated version, two organizational systems are found rather consistently. The first pattern can be seen in the Kandel, Swerdlow, Hoffman, and Yablonsky manuscripts, where the medleys are divided into "shers," which might be thought of as pieces comprising two to five sections (as is also true of European freylekhs). The shers are usually at least thirty-two measures long, including repeats. Although musicians did not always agree as to how many sections constituted each sher, one can always find an internal musical logic that seems to bind the sections together into these larger units. A sher might draw its unifying structure from its development of particular motives or gestures, the recurrence of certain cadential figures, or its gradual unfolding of registers.

Roughly two shers correspond to each cycle of the dance. Several additional shers were always needed for the collective promenade and chain ("threading the needle"). The older manuscripts are, in fact, liberally sprinkled with *da capo* (from the beginning) signs, indicating that bandleaders often repeated each sher in its entirety. Nine of the versions I examined contain at least nine shers, and the longest in my collection (Swerdlow 1945) consists of thirteen. The exact length of each sher hardly mattered because, as noted earlier, direct correspondence of phrase length to the dancing was not really an issue. However, musicians did keep their eye on the progress of the dancers, so that they could mark the beginning of the promenade or "threading the needle."

A second pattern can be seen in the Freed, Kostakowsky, Orkin, and Adler/Zeft manuscripts, where the medleys are divided only into short sections separated by double bars. In the Orkin manuscript, the sections are actually labeled as one through twenty-seven. This contrasting method of dividing up the medley can perhaps be traced to the influential sheet music for the sher that Morris Freed published in 1914, which lacked the traditional delineation into multisection entities. It was through the Freed sheet music that the sher became available to everyone (especially novices) on the Jewish wedding music scene. Nevertheless, for the purpose of this study, it is important to consider each complete sher as a unit, because shers have traditionally been multisection entities.

Because so little is known about the traditional sequencing of klezmer tunes (Slobin 2000: 98), this collection is all the more valuable: It offers some of the only hard evidence of how Jewish dance tunes were joined together in medleys. Given so much flexibility with regard to sectional delineation and content—which tunes, how many tunes, how they were sequenced, and which sections varied from manuscript to manuscript, this collection offers clues about how the Russian Sher maintained its overall compositional integrity over the years. One key to its stability was the presence of guideposts within the form that remained relatively consistent throughout the period of my survey. They were placed at the opening section, the Lemisch sher, and the beginning of the New York material, all of which were instantly recognizable by the community.

In the period covered by my study, the music played for the sher was characterized not only by its distinctive melodies but also by tonal relationships that stayed relatively consistent for at least fifty years.[16] As Slobin concluded in *Fiddler on the Move* (2000: 98), the issue of tonality in klezmer music is a tricky one, since there is no one work that deals comprehensively with the complexities of tonal organization in the klezmer repertoire; neither is there any conclusive literature about the similar tonal complexities found in co-territorial celebratory music repertoires (Greek, Romanian, Ukrainian, etc.).[17] Most writers on Jewish folk music have characterized the tradition as being influenced by Eastern and

Balkan modal traditions (such as the Arabic or Turkish makam or the Persian dastgah), but devoid of any fully codified theoretical system (much like the Greek sirta and the Romanian longa).

Nevertheless, these writers have observed that the tonal materials used in klezmer melodies share some of the characteristics of more fully developed modal systems in that they carry extra-musical connotations (happy, mournful, etc.) and use distinctive melodic and cadential formulas. In an essay on what he calls the "altered Dorian" scale, Beregovski (1982) focuses on klezmer melodies' expressive powers, especially in evoking pain and sorrow, and in his work on the klezmer tradition, he makes reference to the principal klezmer "modes" and their characteristic motifs and cadences (Beregovski 2001). Henry Sapoznik and Pete Sokolow regard klezmer "modes" as instrumental derivations of cantorial *shtaygers* (lit. manners, ways, but often translated as "modes") (Sapoznik and Sokolow 1980). Joshua Horowitz combines Beregovski's classifications with cantorial theory, constructing an elaborate system of modes and "submodes," perhaps based on the systems used at Berklee College of Music to classify the melodic language of "modal jazz" (Horowitz 1992). He also explores the idea of "modal interchange," a concept used in Turkish makam theory to describe melodies whose paths stray temporarily out of one makam and into other ones. Joel Rubin (2001) approaches tonal groupings in a manner similar to that used by Karl Signell (1977) in his work on Turkish makam. Mark Slobin (1982, 2000) prefers to avoid any references to traditional modal classification other than major and minor, but instead considers each melody as a unique collection of pitches. Peter Manuel (1989) discusses the use of "mode" and harmony in various syncretic Eastern European popular musics, including klezmer. All of these authors make some reference to the fairly large body of work on the modal language of cantorial music summarized in Idelsohn (1929), Avenary (1972, 1979), Levine (1981), and Cohen (2000: 281–295). Still, none of this literature paints a complete picture of the Jewish cantorial tradition in its Eastern European context and, except for identifying basic tonal materials, no writer has uncovered any conclusive evidence of systematic modal practice in klezmer composition.

In looking at the tonal groupings used in Philadelphia's Russian Sher medley and in klezmer music in general, I conclude that, while klezmer musicians never developed a fully codified modal language, they did work within a tonal context that was deeply influenced by both eastern (makam) and western (major and minor) modal systems and that, for the purpose of clarity in musical analysis, it does make sense to use terminology from within both of those systems as reference points. Yet, the klezmorim I interviewed used only two terms to refer to the tonal language of their dance tunes: major and minor, occasionally mentioning what they called "Jewish minor." They used the term "major" to refer to western major scales (hereafter labeled as Maj1) or typical Romanian pitch groupings that include the major scale's lower pentachord with an altered upper tetrachord (hereafter labeled as Maj2).[18] Prominent tonal groupings found in the Philadelphia Russian Sher medley are outlined in Figure 5.5, along with examples corresponding to each grouping.

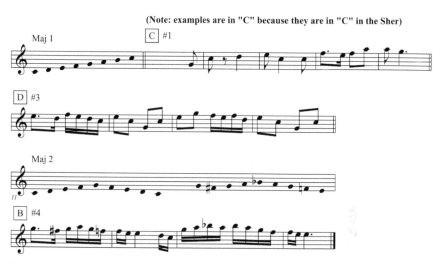

Figure 5.5. Two major tonal groupings, along with corresponding melodic fragments.

Klezmorim used the term "minor" to refer to tunes in harmonic minor (labeled as mi1), melodic minor (labeled as mi2), a hybrid extended melodic minor with a lowered ninth degree (labeled as mi3), and a minor scale with a raised fourth degree, similar to the pitches used in the Turkish makam nikriz, a tonality that Beregovski calls "altered Dorian"[19] (labeled as mi4); in other words, to label any tune that they might accompany with a minor chord. These four minor tonal groupings, along with examples of corresponding melodic fragments from Philadelphia's Russian Sher medley, are shown in Figure 5.6.

Figure 5.6. Four minor tonal groupings, along with corresponding melodic fragments from Philadelphia's Russian Sher medley.

Another pitch collection prominently featured in Philadelphia's Russian Sher medley is what European klezmorim were known to call freygish (Figure 5.7).[20] It uses pitch material related to makam hijaz, a sound also heard frequently in Greek and Balkan dance music and folksong. Some klezmorim think of it as a harmonic minor scale starting on the fifth degree, while others consider it an altered form of a major scale, since they would normally harmonize it with a major chord.

Figure 5.7. Pitch collection known as "freygish."

Scholars (Beregovski 2000; Rubin 2001) have also observed that klezmer melodies often contain cadential figures comprised of tonal groupings that are outside the phrase's primary pitch collection, while other figures stay within the prevailing tonality. Figure 5.8 shows cadential passages corresponding to phrases in the various tonalities found in the Philadelphia Russian Sher medley.

In addition, there are a number of "signal" figures and melodic figures in some of the minor sections that bring in the sound of a natural sixth (a tone

Figure 5.8. Cadential passages.

Figure 5.9. "Signal" figures in the minor sections that bring in the sound of a natural sixth.

outside any of the pitch collections outlined earlier) below the tonal center (Figure 5.9).

Finally, other tonal irregularities often find their way into the music, especially in passages where melodic gesture seems more important than any particular collection of pitches. In this analysis I do my best to consider each melody individually with an ear toward gestural language, while taking note of unique melodic moves and tonal shifts.

The tonal centers found within the most complete renditions of the Philadelphia Russian Sher medley over a period of at least fifty years are remarkably consistent. As early as 1918 (the date of the Kandel recording), four distinct tonal centers, which may be defined as sections with a definite tonic or resolution point and collections of pitches that imply scales or other modal material, divide the piece clearly into four parts:

Part 1: Shers in various forms of A minor
Part 2: Shers that are mostly in A freygish
Part 3: Shers in various types of D minor (usually corresponding to the promenade section of the dance)
Part 4: Shers in D freygish or after 1940 "Der Nayer Sher" (The New Sher, a 1940 Abe Ellstein composition), a composition in D Maj1 and D Maj2

On listening to the medley, one can easily hear the tonal logic of such a structure, and its sequence may show the influence of western musical formulas.[21] However, it could just as well reflect the influence of modal systems such as Turkish makam, in which similar modulations are not uncommon.[22]

In examples spanning the period 1914 to 1968, the length of each part of the sher varies widely. As early as the 1920s we can see a pattern emerging—the A minor part becomes shorter, the A freygish part grows, and the D minor part becomes much longer. A proportional breakdown of the sher medleys grouped by key center and tonality, using seven of the examples I collected, shows the variations and the general pattern (Figure 5.10).

Why does the A minor part shrink? This has an older character, is more tonally complex, and seems more tightly constructed in comparison to the other sections. It is also essentially old-time European Jewish fiddle music (see the later discussion). Short of a 1940s traditionalist revival, mid-twentieth-century American musicians were highly unlikely to come up with more material of this

Freed 1914	A minor			A freygish	D minor	
M. Swerdlow 1914	A minor		A freygish		D minor	
Hoffman 1927	A minor	A freygish	D minor	D freygish	D minor	D Frey.
H. Swerdlow 1945	A minor	A frey.	A mi.	A frey.	D minor	D major
Orkin 1950s	A minor	A frey.	A mi.	A frey.	D minor	D major
Yablonsky 1960	A minor	A frey.	A mi.	A frey.	D minor	D major
Adler/Zeft 1968	A minor	D minor			D mi.	A mi.	D major

Figure 5.10. Seven examples of sher medleys showing the emergence of a general proportional pattern of key centers emerging over time.

sort and the American audience would not tend to favor it. At the same time, it was easier for the younger generation to find or compose newer and more modular material in A freygish, D major, and D minor.[23]

As the older generation, the "keepers of the guard" for the Philadelphia klezmer tradition, faded away, the D minor section (mostly material from the New York Russian Sher medley) grew and eventually came to dominate the medley. As we see in more detail later, as the community (audience and musicians) became more cosmopolitan, the piece lost much of its provincial uniqueness.

Structure

The preceding sectional analysis reveals the historical unfolding of the Philadelphia Russian Sher medley by showing the compositional considerations of musicians of different generations, as reflected in their approaches to tonality. I now examine each of the four parts of the medley, focusing on arranging, harmonic progression, style, performance practice, and what the music of each part reveals about its historical context. I divide each part of the medley into shers (Freed #1, etc.), each sher into sections (A, B, C), and each section into phrases as needed.

Part 1: The A Minor Shers

The A minor shers form a tightly interwoven unified dance medley that sounds as if it might have been written by one composer. As the opening part of the Philadelphia Russian Sher medley, these shers also have a special significance for both the musicians and their audience: They contain the fanfare that serves as the "signal," the signature phrase that immediately tells the audience that a sher is about to begin. It is a phrase that links generations and registers with the Philadelphia audience in an almost Pavlovian way: It says, "Find your partner and get ready to dance!" (Figure 5.11).

The opening sections of the shers in Part 1 all center around A minor and C major, with the sections in minor fluctuating between an mi1 sound and an

Figure 5.11. Part 1: A minor shers.

mi3 sound and the major sections fluctuating between Maj1 and Ma2. The first four bars of sher #1, sections A and C, feature declamatory military-style phrases, followed by a sixteenth note figure that winds its way down to the cadence. This sixteenth note figure appears four times in Part 1 and seems to be a stock phrase that klezmorim of Freed's vintage might have often encountered, although its lowered ninth scale degree is definitely more characteristic of older klezmer tunes, such as the Abe Schwartz freylekhs transcribed in Figure 5.12.

Figure 5.12. Sixteenth-note figure from Part 1 of the Philadelphia Russian Sher medley compared with the melody of a freylekhs recorded by Abe and Sylvia Schwartz in 1920.

Because of the vintage nature of the A minor material, it is perhaps worth looking at how the tunes found here conform to the characterization of Jewish dance melodies by Beregovski (2001: 11) in *Jewish Instrumental Folk Music:*

> The range of small-part compositions is usually within an octave to a tenth, but certain sections are often played or repeated an octave higher, broadening the range of the whole piece. Melodically, intervals of more than a fourth or fifth are rare; generally, development is gradual. Sequential motion in a motif descending to the tonic is common enough, while triadic motion is rare. Most commonly, things move along with sixteenth and eighth notes (at faster tempos), with frequent syncopated rhythms.

Looking at the A minor shers, we can quickly see the ways in which they conform and do not conform to Beregovski's rules. While sixteenth notes, eighth notes, sequential motion, and syncopated rhythms do figure prominently, the first and second measures of the shers contain both octave leaps and triads, and the second strain quickly extends the range up to a twelfth. Yet, with all of their leaps and registral probing, almost every section of the first four shers returns faithfully to the opening A tonic in its final cadence, moving to it in every case down a minor third from the C directly above it (Figure 5.13).

The motivic material in the A minor shers is very much of a piece. There are three easily discernible types of melodies here: declamatory figures (see Figure 5.14), transitional interludes (see Figure 5.15), and scalar strings of sixteenths (see Figure 5.16). In addition, a few significant thematic motives, including a recurring hammered perfect fourth (Figure 5.17) and a syncopated rhythmic figure (Figure 5.18), develop over the course of all four A minor shers.

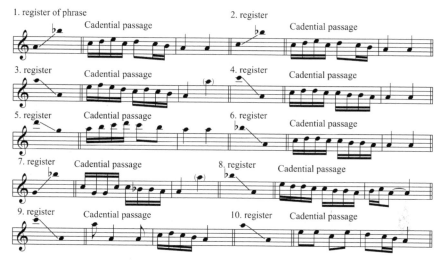

Figure 5.13. Use of register and corresponding cadential passages in the A minor shers.

Figure 5.14. Declamatory figures.

Figure 5.15. Transitional interludes.

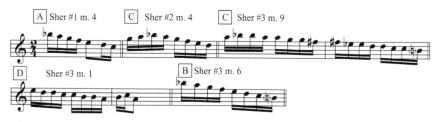

Figure 5.16. Scalar strings of sixteenth notes.

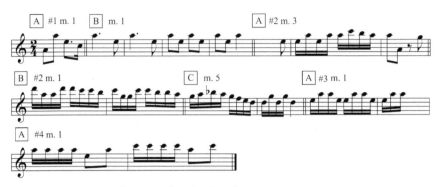

Figure 5.17. A recurring hammered perfect fourth.

Figure 5.18. A syncopated rhythmic figure.

As the dance goes on, several of the phrases are introduced by four-bar signal figures: These occur in sher #2, section A; sher #2, section B; and sher #3, section B. The mi3 tonal grouping appears after the signal figures in sher #2, section A and sher #3, section B; in sher #3, section C, it leads into a rapidly shifting tonal landscape that would be impossible to categorize within any conventional modal system (Figure 5.19).

One of the C major interludes (A minor sher #3, section D) is characterized by two-bar phrases reminiscent of the popular Russian Cossack dance (kozachok) (see Kammen 1924; Figure 5.20).

Part 1 actually has had tremendous longevity. Three of the four A minor shers in Morris Freed's 1914 sheet music edition can still be found in manuscripts from the 1940s and 1950s and in the Yablonsky (Music Associates) manuscript of the early 1960s, making this part, at least in theory, the medley's most stable part. Moreover, no new material of this type seems to have been added at any later date.

Figure 5.19. Scalar passages with rapidly shifting tonalities in sher #3, section C.

Figure 5.20. Russian Cossack Dance compared with A minor sher #3, section D.

However, transcriptions of recorded versions (for example, Kandel 1918, folio and Adler/Zeft 1968, audio recording) and interviews with musicians (Borock 1997b; Hoffman 1998; Katz 2002) reveal that, in practice, musicians did not always play all of the sections of the A minor sher. Why not? While these A minor shers contain many stock phrases that early twentieth-century klezmorim would have known, their quirky hybrid minor tonalities were not so familiar to American-born club-date musicians, and their phrase structures were, most likely, equally puzzling. In general these old klezmer tunes are really only appropriate as fiddle music: A minor is a much better key for instruments from the string family, all of which have open A strings and enhanced resonance in that key. Wind and brass players prefer music in flat keys, such as F (Dmi) or Bb (Gmi). For a variety of reasons, the violin, which had been the key instrument in European klezmer bands, was overtaken by wind and brass instruments in American klezmer ensembles,[24] so that some of the older repertoire (including these A minor shers) did not really suit the new instrumentation.

My search for a contemporaneous model of early twentieth-century European-style sher performance led me to a recording of one of violinist Joseph Solinski's gentle and subtle concert freylekhs, *Rumenishe Fantasie #3*, a piece with a phrase structure very similar to that of the first A minor sher. In Figure 5.21, the opening and one of the B sections of the Solinski piece are matched up against the opening section and one of the B sections of the A minor part of the sher medley (as it appears in Swerdlow 1945).

Figure 5.21. Joseph Solinski Rumanishe (Romanian) Fantasie #3 compared with the opening of A minor sher #1.

Other musician-scholars had already reached a similar conclusion! Thanks to the work of Walter Zev Feldman, Deborah Strauss, and Jeff Warschauer one can actually hear how the A minor shers might have sounded if played by Solinski and his tsimblist or perhaps by a nineteenth-century string ensemble, such as the family orchestra of Selig Itzik Lemisch.

A minor sher #1 is actually the only sher that is found in every manuscript and recording I collected. For this reason, it is a good barometer of phrasing, rhythmic underpinnings, harmonic accompaniments, ornamentation, and orchestration in Philadelphia's Russian Sher medley over the course of the years covered in this survey. Extant versions of the Philadelphia sher reveal a tradition of "personalized" interpretation characteristic of klezmer music throughout its history and preserved in the notated folios of the late 1800s and early 1900s. Beregovski (1982: 501) remarks that there "will be as many variants as klezmorim who have copied one tune," noting that as soon as a tune was copied, ornaments, turns of phrase, and other new elements would be added, whether in the notation or in the performances based on it. This can be seen in the ways that several Philadelphia performers and copyists interpreted sher #1's very first measure (Figure 5.22).

Figure 5.22. Eight versions of the first two measures of sher #1.

Although all of these are versions of the same melody, no two are exactly alike. Even in the earliest manuscripts, it is uncertain whether the second beat of the first bar should be dotted (note the discrepancy between Freed and Hoffman) or whether it should end with an eighth note or two sixteenth notes. In the second measure, what should one do with the syncopation? Is the third bar a recapitulation of the first bar or a variation that includes an ascending arpeggio?

Musicians answered these questions based on their musical backgrounds, the preferences of the other musicians with whom they played, and their exposure to various musical resources. The way Harry Swerdlow wrote the melody in his book indicates that he was acutely aware of how his European-born father, Meyer, had played it on the violin. When Jerry Adler played it, he seemed to be thinking of the straight rhythms of the Freed sheet music and the crisp military-style phrasing of his partner, trumpeter Morris Zeft. Similarly, a careful look at the B section of sher #1 reveals a variety of possible interpretations (Figure 5.23).

Figure 5.23. B section of sher #1 as it appears in the Freed, Hoffman, Freedman, Swerdlow, and Adler manuscripts and as played by Kandel's orchestra, Sam Freeman with Abe Neff, and Jerry Adler with Morris Zeft.

Choices of where and whether or not to trill, whether to play rhythms dotted or straight, how many pick-up notes to use, which articulations work best, and how to harmonize also reflected one's lineage and training. An obvious point of disagreement (and potential clash, should the wrong two musicians find themselves on the same bandstand) is the final cadence. The choices made by the younger musicians are most probably based on the models set out by their mentors or earlier recordings or sheet music. Sam Freeman, the clarinetist on the Abe Neff recording, may be familiar with the Hoffman version (or perhaps he simply favors chromatic lines), while Jerry Adler almost certainly copies his cadential figure from Morris Freed's printed edition. Meanwhile, the Freedman

Figure 5.23. Continued.

and Swerdlow families are in agreement with Shulem Alexander, the old-time clarinetist on the Kandel recording.

In Harry Kandel's recording of the sher medley, we hear the A minor shers arranged for a relatively large ensemble. This rendition takes us right into the heart of the Philadelphia Jewish wedding music scene of the late 1910s. Many of the musicians heard on this recording were local legends who had great longevity (for a partial listing, see Chapter 2). A transcription of the B section of sher #1 from Kandel's recording reveals the interaction of these musicians (Figure 5.24).[25]

While Kandel was indeed a military bandmaster who worked under John Phillip Sousa, few standard concert-band arranging techniques are reflected in

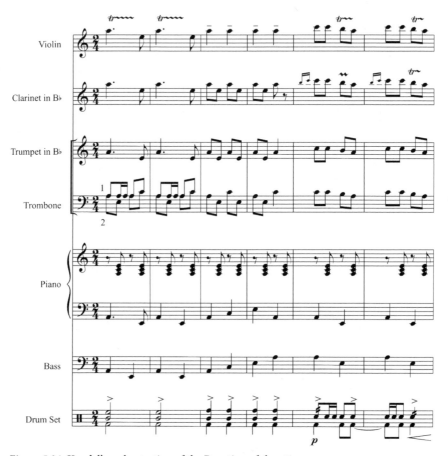

Figure 5.24. Kandel's orchestration of the B section of sher #1.

his rendition of the Philadelphia Sher. There is hardly any use of counterpoint or textual variety, as there would be, for example, in a Sousa march. Instead we hear a great deal of heterophonic unison (a simultaneous layering of the same melody played in contrasting versions) even from the trombone, which in most arrangements would play arpeggiations with a strong rhythmic drive); strings following *secund* (accompaniment) style rhythmic patterns; and percussion providing mostly coloristic underpinnings and accents. This is all in stark contrast to a contemporaneous performance by New York bandleader Abe Schwartz, whose band takes a decidedly more raucous approach. Both Schwartz and Kandel replace the old-world drones and *Alberti*-style accompaniment of the Freed sheet music (credited as the source on the Schwartz 78s) with "um-chick" (alternating bass chord) accompaniment and a more westernized approach to harmonic motion; for example, the IV–V–I progression beginning in the tenth bar of sher #1, section B, and the dominant chord inserted in the third measure

Figure 5.24. Continued.

of sher #2, section B. Figure 5.25 contrasts some of the harmonies in the Schwartz version with the corresponding sections in Freed's manuscript.

In later recordings, however, the spirit does turn more consistently raucous, and in all likelihood, this would also have been the case in much earlier performances, not preserved on recordings, when musicians played the Philadelphia Russian Sher medley for dancers. The exact rhythms of the 1914 Freed sheet music can still be heard on a live recording made in June 1968 at the annual dance of a B'nai Brith lodge. Here we have an example of the most typical instrumentation for a four-piece Jewish band in the 1950s and 1960s. The band consists of four musicians: clarinetist Jerry Adler, trumpeter Morris Zeft, pianist Sam Zager, and drummer Jack Shapiro. By this point in time, the violins are all but irrelevant; were it a five-piece group, a string bass would be added, and were a sixth instrument to be added, it would be a trombone.

The musicians featured in this recording are as old-school Jewish as one might find anywhere in the 1960s. My great-uncle Jerry Adler learned Jewish

Figure 5.25. Contrasts between some harmonies in the Schwartz version with the corresponding sections in Freed's manuscript.

music from the older "klezmer" generation, including my grandfather Kol Katz, whose idiosyncrasies are detailed in the Introduction. Zeft (usually called by his nickname, "Zeftie") started out as an American-style trumpet soloist on Philadelphia radio in the 1930s, but found his way into Jewish music one Sunday morning, when he was drafted as a last-minute replacement for the trumpeter on "Nathan Fleisher's Jewish Hour" by bandleader Bennie Mosicant (Zeft 1981). Since the 1940s (and the departure of Jacob Swerdlow and Mel Davis for New York), Zeft—almost totally blind since the early 1950s—has been considered the top Jewish trumpet player in Philadelphia. Zager, a fine all-around old-time

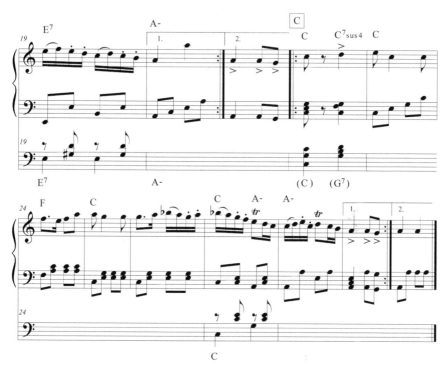

Figure 5.25. Continued.

pianist, was treasurer of the Musicians' Union for many years. Shapiro, proprietor of Jack's Barber Shop in northeast Philadelphia, came to the city from Romania in the 1920s. At the time of this recording (1968), he was still making his own drumheads, using animal skins that he would cure and stretch in his bathtub (Shapiro 1984 pers. comm.). A true connoisseur of Russian military-style drumming, he made klezmer an important component of his teaching method. On the 1968 Adler/Zeft recording, Alan Shapiro, one of Jack's sons, is the emcee, and we hear him call for the signal and announce: "Now, this is a Russian Sher, forty-four verses to play, an old-time scissors dance. Four couples, eight people, here we go!" (Figure 5.26).

Although this sher was recorded in 1968, it stands as a (perhaps unselfconsciously constructed) buffer to the musical ferment of the 1960s. There are no secret- agent–style interludes, no Latin vamps, no funky rhythms, and few modern harmonies, although some chromatic line clichés in the piano part make their way into the mix in measures 5 and 6. The clarinetist and trumpeter know every nuance of each other's phrasing, but have no qualms about occasional heterophony, and the piano is as steady as can be, playing only the most traditional accompaniment figures. These are musicians who know their value as keepers of a flame, bearers of a legacy that is almost gone. Still, this is very

Figure 5.26. B Section of A minor sher #1 as played by the Jack Shapiro ensemble, June 1968.

much American-style klezmer, with piercing clarinet and trumpet and driving, powerful Russian military-style drumming.

The A minor shers ground the Philadelphia Russian Sher medley in old-world march-like freylekhs, with eastern-sounding melodic swirls that twist, turn, and wind around, evoking bold gestures from a pre-harmonic past. These dance tunes are technically demanding and relentless in their busy deedle-deedle rhythms, and no matter what rendition we look at or listen to, they are very much symbolic of a bygone era. Still, they are essential—without them, no medley could be thought of as a Philadelphia Russian Sher.

Part 2: Shers in A Freygish

The beginning of the second part of the sher medley provides a stark contrast to the busy A minor shers just discussed. In Part 2 we find an abrupt switch to material in freygish, the expressive hallmark sound of Hasidic Jewish chants (and a cornerstone of popular Jewish music—think "Hava Nagila" or "If I were a Rich Man") with the instantly recognizable wailing sound preferred by American Jewish ears (Figure 5.27).

This section of the sher underwent a large-scale change in the 1930s and 1940s as a new generation of musicians with less awareness of Middle Eastern–influenced modal traditions crafted new material. In an era when hall weddings gave way to functions held at more modern synagogues and catering houses, many of this part's European sher melodies were displaced

Figure 5.27. Part 2: Shers in A freygish.

Part 2, p. 2 (Shers in A Freygish)
Sher # 6 (Swerdlow 1914, Freed 1914)

Also, Sections C + D can be found in Music Associates
1960s as the C+D sections of Sher #4

Figure 5.27. Continued.

by more streamlined, brassy Odessa-style tunes, tunes that also fit better on the clarinet and trumpet that came to dominate the front line. The audience presumably liked the change too; these were the kinds of Jewish dance tunes American Jewish audiences of this generation preferred (and still prefer) to dance to.[26]

In almost every version I collected, the first phrase of the freygish part is modeled after a section of one of the Lemisch shers dating to the late nineteenth

Part 2, p. 3, Philadelphia Russian Sher Medley (A Freygish Shers)
Sher #7 - Freed

Sher #8 Freed 1914, Swerdlow. 1914
Sher # (?) Kandel, ca 1910

Figure 5.27. Continued.

century. As mentioned earlier, this sher may have been among the first to arrive
in Philadelphia. While motivic development in Part 2 continues along the lines
of Part 1, the gradual stepwise unfolding of the register, a characteristic typical
of older freygish melodies, is the most pronounced compositional feature of
this section.

In his exploration of Jewish prayer modes, pioneering Jewish ethnomusi-
cologist Avraham Zvi Idelsohn looked to eastern modal systems (especially
Arabic and Turkish musics) for clues as to how Jewish music might be analyzed.
He comments on the formalized unfolding of freygish as it manifests itself in

cantorial expression: "The resting points of the motives are: the fourth, the seventh below the tonic, the third, and the tonic. . . . It climbs in tetrachordal (four note) curves, first to the fourth" (Idelsohn 1929: 88). He goes on to discuss the mode's tendency to tonicize (resolve to) the fourth degree. Karl Signell (1977: 79) has pointed out similar tendencies in makam hijaz, a prominent Turkish modal sound and a likely influence on Jewish material in freygish. Figure 5.28 illustrates the registral motion in the first A freygish sher.

Figure 5.28. Registral motion in the first A freygish sher.

One of the clear goals in the registral movement in Morris Freed shers 5 and 6 is to achieve a gradual resolution from A freygish to D minor with a raised fourth degree (mi4). These resolutions occur at the beginning of each C section (Figure 5.29).

Figure 5.29. Resolutions to D minor occurring at the beginning of each C section.

Later manuscripts also linger for a while in A freygish, but do so using material with little resemblance to that found in the Freed version. The version found in the 1946 Swerdlow folio provides a window into the kind of material preferred by Philadelphia klezmorim of the 1940s (Figure 5.30).

While the newer tunes use much of the same pitch material as Freed shers #6, #7, and #8, they lack both the formalized gradual registral unfolding that often characterizes Middle Eastern and Jewish music with a hijaz sound and its tendency toward resolution and modulation to a minor tonality a fourth above. Instead, they feature quick moves from A freygish down to G major (Maj1) and then, through a typical cadential formula (implying G minor), back to A freygish (as in Swerdlow [1945] shers #5 and #8; Figure 5.31).

While the slow scalar development is gone, there is still tremendous strength in the sequencing of the new material. Each tune ends with a motive that leads

Part 2, p. 4 ("A Freygish" Shers) Phila. Russian Sher Medley from more recent folios
Sher #5 (in Adler 1940's Swerd. 1945, Orkin 1950's, Ma. 1960's)

Sher #6 (in Adler 1940's, Swerd. 1945, Orkin 1950's, Ma 1960's)

Sher #7 (Swerd, 1945, Orkin 1950's Ma 1960's)

Sher #8 (in Swerdlow 1945, Orkin 1950's)
(#7 in Adler 1940's)

This Bulgar is also found as Sher #6 (transposed to "D") in Hoffman 1927

Figure 5.30. A Freygish shers found in later manuscripts.

Figure 5.31. A typical G minor to A freygish cadential figure.

seamlessly into the next sher, not unlike the motivic continuity found in many jazz solos. In the new sequence, the concluding motive of Swerdlow (1945) sher #5 becomes the beginning motive of Swerdlow (1945) sher #6 (Figure 5.32).[27]

Figure 5.32. Ending cadential motive of Swerdlow (1945) sher #5 as opening motive of Swerdlow (1945) sher #6.

Similarly, a rhythmic phrase at the end of Swerdlow sher #6 becomes the rhythmic phrase that starts Swerdlow sher #7. This sher also marks an unexpected return to A minor (mi4) and C major (Maj2) (Figure 5.33).

Figure 5.33. Rhythmic figure that ends Swerdlow (1945) sher #6 and also begins sher #7.

Finally, sher # 8 brings in a freygish melody with the same phrase structure as the previous minor tune[28] (Figure 5.34).

Figure 5.34. Freygish melody with the same phrase structure as the previous minor tune.

There are also important differences in rhythm and phrasing that distinguish these shers from the earlier ones. The second A freygish sher in this manuscript (#5 in the Swerdlow book) features four-bar phrases that revolve around quarter notes, which contrast with the two-bar phrases that are so pronounced in the earlier manuscripts. Also gone are the dotted eighth-sixteenth rhythms and small syncopations found in the older shers. In general, the new material is far less technically demanding.

Some of these two-section tunes are so different from the older three- and four-section sher melodies because they are actually bulgars. In an article on the roots and American transformation of the bulgar, Feldman distinguishes older Jewish dances (such as the sher) from the bulgar, a late nineteenth-century Bessarabian development that became transformed again in its American incarnation:

> Apart from modal and melodic differences, both the sirba and the bulgareasca were rhythmically differentiated from the core klezmer dance repertoire due to the presence of triplets. . . . The bulgareasca alternates triplets with syncopated phrases, often using eighth note/quarter note/eighth note patterns, with frequent held notes of a half note duration or more. (Feldman 2002: 98)

As Feldman (2002: 112) also points out, for Jewish American musicians and patrons of the 1940s generation, the distinction between shers and bulgars had been lost; in the new climate even Dave Tarras was creating mostly freylekhs/bulgar hybrids. One of these hybrid tunes is shown in Figure 5.35 (part of Swerdlow sher #5), which begins as a traditional sher with a familiar eighth-eighth-quarter motif, culminating in a more bulgar-like construction.

Figure 5.35. Melody with sher-like opening, morphing into a bulgar after four measures.

A close look at other folios reveals some of the possible sources for at least two of these "new" bulgar-like shers, and, as it turns out, they appear on the scene much earlier than one might think. Sher #6 in Swerdlow (1945) can be found as early as 1914 (as sher #7 in Meyer Swerdlow's cornet folio of that year), while sher #8 from Swerdlow (1945) also appears (in D freygish) as sher #6 in veteran musician Joseph Hoffman's 1927 folio. Their presence in these vintage folios signifies the tacit acceptance (at least by the compiler) of changes that must have been in the making on the bandstand for years before. Then, over time, the new tunes spread until the changes become ubiquitous, and by the 1940s one finds few traces of the earlier A freygish shers.[29]

The material in Swerdlow's 1945 folio is terse and catchy, more like short individual tunes than sections of a traditional sher. Completely devoid of the deedle-deedle sixteenth-note figures identified with the old-world freylekhs of the Freed 1914 edition, these melodies have a brash and modern physicality to them. Flaunting the rules of European sher construction, they signify that a new American-born generation has taken over for good.

Part 3: Shers in D Minor (including the New York Russian Sher Medley)

The D minor section of the Philadelphia Russian Sher medley might be seen as a harbinger of encroaching cosmopolitanism—as just another manifestation of the ever-growing influence of New York on America's provincial Jewish communities. As noted earlier the D minor section tends to grow and grow over the years, even more profoundly in live performance than it does in manuscript versions. One can hardly blame the musicians and audience for succumbing to the foreign power: The New York Russian Sher medley (here beginning with Swerdlow [1914], sher #9) is extremely catchy, and its first few strains are interwoven with an intricate compositional logic. Its later inclusion of popular Second Avenue Yiddish theater tunes is another plus in an American environment where audiences crave the familiar (Figure 5.36).

As I previously mentioned, a D minor tonality is foreshadowed in all of the A freygish shers found in the older manuscripts (Freed 1914 and Swerdlow 1914). The final A freygish sher in the Freed sheet music progresses quickly to a D minor tonic, staying there for sections B, C, and D and finally ending in D. The newer manuscripts reveal a much more dramatic move to D: All of the newer A freygish shers stay in an A tonality, putting off any resolution to D until Part 3 begins.

Once Part 3 does start, there is no consensus as to what sequence should be followed. Four of the manuscripts (Hoffman 1927, Swerdlow 1945, Orkin 1950s, Adler) begin with a freylekhs in mi3 (Figure 5.37).

Other manuscripts (including Swerdlow 1914) move directly into material also found in the New York Russian Sher medley (Figure 5.38).

Once the "New York" sher material has been exhausted, the actual sequencing here has an improvisational quality, and each sher's length varies. Different versions might lead into a popular adesa bulgar (bulgar from Odessa); an early twentieth-century Yiddish theater melody, *"Ikh bin a border bay mayn vayb"* (I Am a Lodger at My Wife's Place), and the Yiddish folksong, *"Ikh bin shoyn a meydl In di yorn"* (I am a Girl Already Advanced in Years). All of these tunes were also popular among New York musicians.

Over time, Philadelphia's klezmorim gave increasing weight to the New York material and approach. In a 1968 recording by the Jack Shapiro Orchestra, featuring clarinetist Jerry Adler and trumpeter Morris Zeft, musicians—who in previous years might have played many more of the earlier strains—take a left turn immediately after the very first A minor sher of Part 1 (which they play twice), skipping the A freygish shers of Part 2 altogether, and head straight for

The Phila. Russian Sher Medley, Part 3, The D Minor Shers
Sher #9 (in Swerdlow 1945, Orkin.1950's, Sher #10 in Swerdlow 1914, Sher #4 in Hoffman 1927, Sher #5 in Kandel 1918, Sher # 8 in Adler 1940s and Music Associates 1960s)

Sher #5 (in Hoffman 1927)
(Ikh Bin A Border Bay Mayn Vayb)

Sher #10 (in Swerdlow 1945)
Sher #4 (in Adler 1968). Also known as a popular Adeser Bulgar (dance from Odessa).

Figure 5.36. Part 3: Shers in D minor, including the New York Russian Sher medley.

Philadelphia Russian Sher Medley, Part 3, More D Minor Shers

Sher #9 (Swerdlow 1914), Sher #7 (Hoffman 1927), Sher #4 (Kandel 1918), Sher #8 (Orkin 1950's,
Music Associates 1960's), Sher #11 (Swerdlow 1945), Sher #10 (Adler 1940's) Sher #1 (Kammen Book #1, NY 1920s)

Sher #12 Swerdlow 1945), Sher #5 (Adler 1968) Ikh Bin Shoyn A Meydl in di Yorn (I Am A Girl Already Advanced in Years)

Figure 5.36. Continued.

the D minor world of New York, making what seems like a rather jarring modulation (Figure 5.39).

In this rendition, we hear an improvised medley as it unfolds. After opening with the second section of the New York Sher and moving on to the usual adeser bulgar and "Ikh bin shoyn a meydl in di yorn," the musicians follow with a medley of popular Jewish melodies, including "*A khulem*" (A Dream) and "*Undzer rebenyu*" (Our Rabbi); (two well-known folk tunes), "*Vu zaynen mayne zibn gute*

Philadelphia Russian Sher Medley, Part 3, More D Minor Shers

Sher #13 (Swerdlow 1945), Sher #3 (Adler 1968), Sher #10 (Music Associates), Sher #9 (Orkin 1950's)
Sher #11 (Adler 1940's), Sher #2 (Kammen Book, N.Y, 1920s)

Sher #6 (in Adler 1968) *Vu Zaynen Mavne Zibn Gute Yor?* (Where Are My Seven Good Years?), *A Khulem* (A Dream)

Figure 5.36. Continued.

yor?" (Where Are My Seven Good Years); a popular Yiddish theater song; and a Bessarabian bulgar. This musical snapshot reveals the signaling that takes place on the bandstand when the order of a medley is not predetermined.

From the outset Zeft, the trumpeter, is leading and the others are doing their best to follow. The first conflict happens at the end of sher #2 when Morris Zeft moves on to the adeser bulgar, and Jerry Adler attempts to continue with the traditional New York medley (Figure 5.40). Another clash occurs in sher #4, when Zeft fumbles for a few seconds and then goes back to a tune he has already played (Figure 5.41).

Moments like these reveal the kind of fluidity and spontaneity that linked Philadelphia's twentieth-century klezmorim with the musical culture of preceding generations. For these aging musicians, the Jewish culture of their youth was still very much alive. By the time of this recording, however, the folios I collected no longer really reflected current performance practices.

Figure 5.37. Freylekhs in D minor (3).

from Swerdlow 1914

Figure 5.38. Beginning of New York Russian Sher #1.

(#1)

(#2)

Figure 5.39. Final strain of A minor sher #1, heading directly into a D minor sher.

D minor Sher - clarinet signals next section of sher, trumpet leads into bulgar.

Adler

Zeft

Figure 5.40. Two lead players start moving in different directions, but the clarinetist immediately defers to the trumpeter.

End of "Zibn gite yor"   Normal beginning of phrase   A Khulem (reprise in new key)

D-   (A min)

Figure 5.41. Both lead players hesitate at the beginning of a new section.

Part 4: Freylekhs in D Freygish and "Der Nayer Sher" (The New Sher), a Bulgar in D Major

Part 4 of the Philadelphia Russian Sher medley moves the music from D minor into a D freygish (or major) tonality[30] and corresponds to that part of the dance where guests form a chain and "thread the needle." This final move is the last link in the progression of resolutions that lead up to it, and musically, it feels very much like an arrival. In later versions, as we see, the arrival not only is the resolution of a tonal journey but also is the culmination of a chronological one: Musically, we head toward the 1940s, the beginning of a very difficult era for immigrant Jewish culture.

In several early manuscripts and recordings (Kostakowsky 1916, Kandel 1921, Hoffman 1927), the Philadelphia Russian Sher medley concludes with a lively freylekhs in freygish, characterized by fanfare-like two-bar phrases in the A section and a march-like B section.[31]

In later manuscripts and recordings (beginning roughly in the 1940s), the freygish melodies are followed or replaced by "Der Nayer Sher" or, as it says in the 1945 Swerdlow folio, by a "Bulgar called *Nayer Sher*" (the latter title echoing Zev Feldman's skepticism about the later generation's ability to differentiate bulgars from shers), a tune set in D Maj2 (Figure 5.42). The tune is a 1940 composition by Juilliard-trained Yiddish theater composer Abraham Ellstein. He reportedly wrote it while riding on a streetcar, on the way to a recording session with Yiddish matinee idol and recording artist Seymour Rechtzeit and the perennially popular Barry Sisters, who were the first artists to record it. Subsequently, it became an English-language hit when several popular American performers (including Eartha Kitt) recorded it as the "Wedding Samba." While it appears in all of the post-1940 manuscripts that I collected, it was generally not incorporated into the sher medley manuscripts, but was found in a different part of the folio as a discrete composition. This way, it could be played, instead of the sher, for audiences who only wanted a hint of the larger medley or for those who knew it as a modern Yiddish or American pop tune (Katz 2003, pers. comm.).

A comparison of the published sheet music version to the transcriptions found in the Swerdlow and Yablonsky folios reveals how quickly "Der Nayer Sher" changed in the hands of dance musicians. While the rhythms of the A section are identical to those on the sheet music, the B section is livened up considerably in the dance version. When comparing "Der Nayer Sher" to the earlier freygish tune, it is also interesting to note some points of rhythmic convergence, particularly in the B section, which could have been a factor in the choice of this work as a substitute for the older tune.

Even if the earlier sections of the medley go by the dancers in a kind of blur, "Der Nayer Sher," a relatively recent popular bulgar/Yiddish American pop tune, brings the dance to an end on a familiar and relatively up-to-date note. Indeed, for most musicians it truly marked the end of the medley—once "Der Nayer Sher" was concluded (and most musicians played only its first two

Part 4- Phila. Russian Sher Medley, Shers in D "Freygish" and Der Nayer Sher (D Major)

Sher #5 (in Kandel 1918), Sher #9 (in Hoffman 1927) Sher #3 (in Kostakowsky 1916)

Sher #7 (in Adler 1968)

Der Nayer Sher (in Adler 1940's, Swerdlow 1945, Orkin 1950's, Music Associates1960's, Adler 1968)

B (B section from original sheet music)

Figure 5.42. Part 4: Freylekhs in D freygish and "Der Nayer Sher" ("The New Sher") by Abraham Ellstein, a Bulgar in D major.

strains), they simply reprised it until the dancers finished, as if to say "enough, already!"

Conclusion

In later years, it became difficult to find the necessary number of knowledgeable guests to do a proper sher, and caterers and emcees often found themselves leading the dance. Trumpeter Marvin Katz pointed out that in the 1960s and 1970s the dance would often end prematurely because of the advanced ages and lack of stamina of the participants. By the 1980s, few musicians could make their way through it in any form, despite the availability of notated versions, and the dance virtually disappeared. Still the memory of its glory days was enough to inspire the inevitable request from the older relative:

> There was always one guy who was gonna bug you. He'd come up and say "Play the sher, play the sher, play the sher." You can't get rid of him, so the only thing to do is to play the song. Well, after about the first four phrases of it, you see that nobody's dancing, so you go right back to the beginning and out. I mean, you're not gonna keep going for another twenty minutes when nobody's dancing. (Portnoy 2000)

Who could really blame such a patron? For those who danced to it in its glory days, the wedding is the sher and the sher is the wedding. To have one without the other is unthinkable.

Over the course of twenty-or-so minutes, the music of Philadelphia's Russian Sher medley winds through a compressed soundscape that ties together sensibilities spanning the entire immigrant era. We can hear musicians working on the bandstand, deciding what to drop and what to keep, what they can and cannot handle technically, what works for the crowd and what does not. Taken as a whole, its parts form an intricately woven tapestry, a significant piece of folk art forged over time through a multigenerational collective vision with its history sedimented in the music itself. Its richly layered form preserves older esthetics even as it innovates toward trends in American popular music, on the one hand, and the internal development of this wedding dance, on the other. It is a cultural centerpiece, a paean to continuity, a vehicle through which dancers and musicians exude pride as they pay tribute to those who came before them, not through a dirge or a prayer, but with a celebratory dance.

Epilogue

Much of what I have written here speaks of klezmer as the music of a community. In *Fiddler on the Move,* Mark Slobin (2000) links his study of the klezmer revival with the efforts of different communities to retrofit klezmer in ways to suit their own purposes. These include use of the tradition as a symbol of a new "self-constructed" Jewish or European identity, as a stimulus for the contemporary artistic imagination, or as functional music for contemporary events and celebrations.

Even when klezmer is placed in a functional role, it can feel less than organic as a component of contemporary celebrations, and its original context may be altered. Such a presentation is often a mixture of European social dances, religious customs, ersatz badkhones, and original shtick. Joe Kurland, a bandleader based in Leverett, Massachusetts, describes teaching dances at Jewish celebrations in his regional community in the 1990s:

> We saw at weddings people had no idea what to dance—I'd go out and help them. When you hire the Wholesale Klezmer Band, you're also hiring someone who's going to teach you how to do a traditional wedding. People have called and said, "We'd like to have Jewish music, but we'd also like to have a pop band for dancing." I'll show you how to dance. You'll be so occupied with Jewish dancing you won't have time for other types of dancing. (quoted in Slobin 2000: 79)

To revive interest in Jewish dancing, the Wholesale Klezmer Band even created a new specialty dance:

There's one dance in particular we tell people about, and often people who come from communities who don't know each other and don't know *yiddishkayt* [traditional Jewish customs]—it's where we weave people. You have the *khusn's* [groom's] family in a line and the *kale's* [bride's] family in a line and you weave them in and out until they don't know who's who and they're all one. It makes people feel really included when we do that. (quoted in Slobin 2000: 79)

While Kurland's efforts to reinvent Jewish dancing seem valiant enough, I must admit that I have trouble equating the sense of community such dances create with the actual feeling of an ethnic celebration. Having been present at many contemporary Jewish weddings with imported dance leaders and finding most of them less than satisfying, I wondered what it might be like instead to reconstitute Philadelphia's tried-and-true 1940s wedding traditions at a contemporary "wedding." The opportunity presented itself in the winter of 2000. That year I was invited to be a staff member at Klezkamp, the original camp-like annual gathering of klezmer enthusiasts, held that year in Cherry Hill, New Jersey, just across the Delaware River from Philadelphia. As the only Philadelphia-born music staffer, I suggested that one of the evenings might include a reenactment of a 1940s Philadelphia-style Jewish wedding, and it was put on the schedule.

Unfortunately, the wedding is not the only event on the program. The evening begins with several Yiddish art song selections and the presentation of an award to an aging former Yiddish radio star; many of the younger participants write off the entire program and head elsewhere. There are several other intrinsic problems, including a nearly total lack of liquor and food. Still, the crowd is substantial and enthusiastic, including around three hundred Klezkampers and another fifty curious visitors from across the river.

Moreover, Klezkamp is really a music event, and the band members are as interesting and distinguished a mix as one could hope to find so many years after the end of klezmer as a staple at mainstream Jewish celebrations. Veteran Philadelphia clarinetist Joe Borock is there, only three days out of the hospital following his heart attack ten days earlier. Joining him are local saxophonist and emcee Bobby Block, percussionist Elaine Hoffman Watts, trumpeter Marvin Katz (my mother's brother), along with three eminent New York wedding musicians: reedmen Paul Pincus and Howie Leess, and pianist Pete Sokolow. Rounding out the group, and representing the "younger" (under 60) generation are vocalist Richard Lenatsky, banjoist Henry Sapoznik, trumpeter Susan Watts (Elaine Watts's daughter), vocalist Judy Bressler and bassist Jim Guttmann from my own professional band, and me.

I let the audience in on our goals for the evening:

We're going to have a wedding. . . . I want the people here to really experience this music. . . . klezmer concerts are one thing, but to experience a celebration is a whole other thing, to experience what the music's really for. . . . I need some volunteers—I need a bride and I need a groom . . . married, unmarried, same sex, different sex, it doesn't matter. (videotape of event from Mark Slobin 2000)

A couple steps forward: Chane and Ted, whose actual wedding had coincidentally taken place at a Klezkamp gathering five years earlier. To set the proper tone, I begin by asking Richard to sing "Because," a familiar staple at 1940s American wedding ceremonies:

Because you come to me with naught save love,
And hold my hand and lift mine eyes above,
A wider world of hope and joy I see,
Because you come to me. (D'Hardelot and Teschemacher 1912)

The Yiddish and klezmer purists in the crowd take a deep breath, and I hold my own breath as I realize that, in this ocean of cutting-edge Jewish ritual, we have entered uncharted waters. As the band prepares to play the recessional, "Khusn kale mazeltov" (Congratulations to the Bride and Groom), a receiving line forms, and Bernie Uhr, a man who has hosted thousands of weddings during his sixty-year career as a caterer, leads the crowd past the bride and groom, preparing them for the Grand March. Next, with a familiar fanfare, the March begins, and everyone parades around the room, as Bernie instructs them to wave and smile as they walk.

I notice a bit of chaos on the bandstand: The New York Musicians have segued into a third section of the tune, unknown to the Philadelphians. Regardless, a mood is starting to build—a feeling of community and, perhaps, of some other time and place.

And now, on to the first freylekhs. As instructed, Chane and Ted begin by dancing only with their "immediate family," but within a few minutes, everyone is out on the floor, and the bride and groom are up on chairs (and this time, it is the New Yorkers who are surprised by the third strain of the music!). It feels like a wedding, but like no wedding I've played before . . .

The first groans of the evening come when I make my next announcement. "We will now rise to sing 'The Star Spangled Banner' and 'Hatikvah.'" Still, good sports that they are, everyone dutifully obliges. Despite some more musical clashes (the Philadelphians play the pre-state version of "Hatikvah," while the New Yorkers strike up the contemporary Israeli version), we all make it to the end. At this moment, I sense that some of our new generation klezmer fans are feeling a bit uncomfortable, if not embarrassed.

I read phony telegrams congratulating Chane and Ted (from Presidents Clinton and Roosevelt), make a standard toast, and lead the band in two concert sets that would normally correspond to the serving and eating of the soup. In the first, we feature Joe Borock playing his favorite Yiddish theater and folksong medley: "Mayn tayre" (My Dear One), "Chiribim, chiribum," "Az der rebe Elimeylekh" (When Rabbi Elimylekh), and "Papirosn" (Cigarettes). People sing and clap along. Our second concert-feature is an extraordinary New York-style treat, a doyne featuring Julliard-trained virtuoso Paul Pincus on the clarinet. Now the crowd's attention is riveted to the bandstand.

We lead back into the dancing with a broyges tants (dance of anger and reconciliation), and several couples get right into the spirit, stalking each other angrily. Others gingerly balance bottles on their heads, causing the wedding's focus to dissipate a bit. Just then bandleader Bobby Block comes forward to lead an old-fashioned krinsl (mezinke) ceremony, a ritual that will take its place as the centerpiece of the evening.

After assembling several makeshift families (being careful to jot down a detailed chart of names and family relationships), Block seats the "parents" in four chairs in the center of the room and begins by instructing the "siblings": "When you hear your names, walk up to the four parents, kiss them, congratu-late them, give them a mazel tov, and stand in back of them." The band begins a deliberate version of "Di mezinke iz oysgegebn" (The Youngest Daughter Is Mar-ried Off), and Block addresses the crowd:

> Now, ladies and gentlemen, as you know, there is an old Jewish custom that says, on the night of a mother's last child's marriage, she is to be crowned, just as a queen is crowned. The crown is made of flowers. The flowers symbolize the sweetness of motherhood. And tonight, with Chane and Ted being married, Libby and Blanche are going to be crowned as such. And so, at this time, we would like to call upon the children of both Libby and Motke and Blanche and Yosl [none other than the afore-mentioned Joe Kurland], because we now have a brand-new family that's being formed by this very beautiful marriage. So, won't you welcome the children as they come out to congratulate their parents, beginning with the beautiful sister of our bride, Sore, and her handsome husband, Avrom!

The band crescendos, and I can feel the crowd get in tune with the deliber-ate, formal pageantry that is taking place. The "children" kiss the "parents," the other set of "children" are introduced and do the same, and the spirit builds. Bobby Block announces,

> Ladies and gentlemen, we are now ready for our guests of honor, our stars of the evening. Please welcome Chane and Ted!

The music becomes a bit louder and even more deliberate, and our bride and groom dance in, dramatically holding the krinsls, delicate crowns composed of small white flowers. They place them on the heads of their "mothers," the music stops, and Block asks Libby and Blanche to rise, step forward, and *drey zikh arum a bisl* (turn around a few times), so that those in the back of the hall "might see how lovely you look." There are hugs and kisses all around, the crowd gives them a big hand, and while they take their seats, Block turns his attention to Motke, the "father" of the bride:

> Motke, we are going to give you the singular honor of congratulating your *mekhuteyneste* [sister-in-law] on being crowned. But Motke, do it right!

Motke gives a toast in Yiddish congratulating Blanche, and as he finishes Block starts in again:

> Motke, you'd better take your seat for this, because it seems to me that Yosl is getting a little *broyges* [angry]. We're going to get even with Motke, we're going to ask you to congratulate Libby. But Yosl, do it right!

Now Yosl gives a far more ornate toast, everyone cheers, the chairs are taken away, and the wedding party is invited into the circle. The band strikes up the lively conclusion of the krinsl medley: "Ot azoy, tantsn mit di shviger" (That's the Way to Dance with the Mother-in-Law); "Oy, a sheyne kale" (Oh, a Beautiful Bride), which Block sings; "Mekhuteyneste mayne" (My Dear In-Law), and finally the "Patsh tants" (Hand-Clapping Dance). The ceremony has taken twenty-five minutes and created a blend of music and community spirit beyond anything I have ever experienced. And it is only now, after watching Block lead the krinsl that I finally grasp the true meaning of the phrase "master of ceremonies."

As an aside, I ask Paul Pincus how long a krinsl ceremony would have taken in New York. "Five minutes," is his answer. "So, what do think of what we just did?" I ask. "The musicians must get a lot of overtime down here," is his answer.

We decide to table the Russian Sher until the next morning and conclude the evening with "Platsh Yisroel," Philadelphia's good night waltz. The couples pair up and melt into the music, savoring the moment before it is time to reenter the postmodern world of the klezmer revival.

I also take a moment to revel in my own experience of the evening, particularly the feeling of the krinsl ceremony. Looking back, I could see such a ceremony as a kind of Bakhtinian chronotope, something that simultaneously conjures up diverse eras and feelings. To Bobby Block, it is a ceremony he still performs at every wedding in which a youngest child is involved. To some in the crowd, it is an outmoded ritual that takes the focus away from the intrinsic value of the music itself. For me it is a place where the meaning of my research comes alive: a point of validation, a place where history interacts with present-day reality, brushes against it, and perhaps changes it ever so slightly.

It is at this intersection, where history meets nostalgia, that I conclude. After sifting through the rubble of American klezmer, I believe the genre reveals a deeper meaning when considered apart from the world of virtuosic recordings and glitzy stage shows. Celebration in a community is the true wellspring of klezmer, the process that produced that object, which, these days, is so often recontextualized. A close look at klezmer in its original context (albeit a context that was strained to the limit in the United States) allows one to come to terms with the true face of the music, devoid of any marketing ploy or egocentric spin. It is here where klezmer music has etched its own well-deserved place in American Jewish culture, where we are reminded that how a people celebrates is as much a part of their history as anything else.

I believe klezmer has come back not only because of its catchy tunes and interesting dances but also because of the enduring relevance of such celebrations within Jewish society. To paraphase Archie Green, whose work linked the enduring English ballads of Appalachia with leftist-folksong revivalist aesthetics, ultimately a repertoire is relevant because it is a looking glass reflecting the joys and sorrows, aspirations and fears, of a community (Greene 1966). Likewise, contemporary klezmer has evolved in a way that mirrors modern-day feelings and values. Still, to truly understand the music one must look to its history, to the wedding musician's place in society, to the values the music has expressed, and to the deep feelings the music brings forth when its traditional role is acknowledged and given expression. It is then, when one can feel it and taste it, that klezmer truly comes to life.

I hope this study of Philadelphia's klezmer community will inspire others to look into the history of klezmer traditions in their own communities before these traditions disappear entirely. With so many older musicians now willing to reveal the secrets of their heritage, a vast historical and cultural legacy waits to be uncovered.

Notes

INTRODUCTION

1. Klezmer aficionados date the period of resurgence to the first "revival" recording by *The Klezmorim* in 1977, the same year that a pioneer of the klezmer revival, Henry Sapoznik, began reexploring his Jewish roots (Sapoznik 1999). However, it is now clear that at least a dozen other revival figures, including Stuart Brotman, Michael Alpert, Walter Zev Feldman, and Andy Statman, were exploring klezmer in the early 1970s.

2. Most studies of American Jewish culture focus on New York; a study of Philadelphia's contrasting klezmer tradition can help make an argument for more emphasis on regional studies.

3. My great-grandfather, Shimen Katz, widely known by his nickname *Shayke-lets* ("Little Simon, the comedian") was a wedding entertainer and Yiddish actor in Lemberg, (Lvov) Galicia (now Ukraine), and later in Kishinev, Bessarabia (now Moldova). My grandfather, Kol Katz, worked as a bandleader in Philadelphia from approximately 1920 until his death in 1959. Two of my uncles and two great-uncles also had careers as Jewish wedding musicians.

4. He was referring to one of two possible Motown acts, the "Temptations," a five-man singing group, or the "Four Tops." The fact that he confused the two names is telling, but not surprising, considering his lack of any actual connection (other than professional) to the popular music scene of the 1960s and 1970s.

5. "C" clarinets are seldom used for anything but ethnic music, and Jerry's preference of the Albert system over the much more popular and modern Boehm system marked him as a klezmer throughout his career.

6. Borock's film, titled *A Joyful Noise*, had its first preview in 1997.

7. My most poignant encounter with this double standard occurred at a December 1996 event hosted by Steven Spielberg's Shoah Foundation. Seven musicians from the "revitalization" generation backed up Itzhak Perlman, the featured act, following a cocktail hour

where veteran klezmer clarinet virtuoso Ray Musiker performed background music. Even Perlman commented on the irony.

8. Ethnomusicologist Moshe Beregovski was spurred on by a similar (albeit Soviet-inspired) feeling when he published his first klezmer pamphlet in 1937: "The forms of music-making among professional and amateur musicians have changed radically, and klezmorim—like many of the old order—are entering the realm of the past. But they are not departing the arena of history without a trace. They have left us a rich and precious legacy that deserves further study. Among the compositions created by klezmorim are many pearls, true works of art that are the fruit of the labors of highly gifted artists. The best of these works, along with the folk compositions of other peoples, will take their place in the international treasure-house as resplendent monuments of their era. We will give thanks to those unassuming folk musicians and composers who graced the lives of the broad masses with their art and whose work was a faithful companion to the people and a medium for their joys and sorrows." (Beregovski 2001: 36)

9. As Neil Rosenberg aptly points out in *Transforming Tradition,* revivalists inadvertently or purposefully change the context of the music they bring back, reinventing it in their own image; the music thus becomes a medium to foster the overt cultural and political agenda expressed by the revivalists themselves (Rosenberg 1993: 17).

10. For a more extensive discussion of the implications of the klezmer revitalization movement see Slobin 2000.

11. Even among ethnomusicologists there has been very little work done in documenting mainstream American popular culture (Slobin 1982: xvii), a notable exception being Bruce MacLeod's work on club date musicians (MacLeod 1979, 1992).

12. Such a narrative figures prominently in Sapoznik 1999.

13. I use the male pronoun because the overwhelming majority of older klezmorim were male.

14. In Idelsohn's view, Jewish content was available only in music developed in relatively isolated Middle Eastern communities. In the richly developed German cantorial tradition (born in a region occupied by Jews for more than a thousand years) Idelsohn found "nothing Jewish," and after enumerating a long list of Jewish composers working in popular and classical forms in Europe and America he concluded that none of their work contained "a single element that might be reckoned a Jewish contribution" (Idelsohn 1929: 424).

15. Statements such as this one led Jewish art music scholar Albert Weisser to criticize Beregovski's work on the basis of "narrow dialectical critique and unreliable selectivity" (Weisser 1954: 52). I must confess that the more I read Jewish music studies authors, the more such Marxist points of view resonate for me.

CHAPTER 1

1. Music historian Alfred Sendrey presents a more romanticized notion of Jewish music in biblical times: "As to their social status, the klezmorim and *badkhonim* belonged to the lowest class of Jewish society. . . . What a vast difference when compared to conditions in Biblical times! In the social scheme of Ancient Israel, the itinerant musician was held in high esteem; he was a folkbard, the preserver and dispenser of ancient heroic songs and tales, disseminating good and bad tidings, respected and loved by the people, feared by the rulers. The entire population considered it their duty to provide for their minstrels" (Sendrey 1970: 356). In *Music in Ancient Israel* he writes, "The secular musician in Israel was not the type of a poor and despised wandering minstrel; he never represented the

itinerant miserable profession which in the medieval times brought into discredit popular music" (Sendrey 1969: 544). It is unclear on what sources Sendrey bases these statements.

2. Maimonides is also responsible for the following pronouncement: "Song shall not cross your lips when you drink wine, as it is written: Sing no more while wine is drunk (Lamentations 24: 9), but you may sing to praise God, even under the influence" (Salmen 1991: 25).

3. The non-Jewish world also has a long tradition of suspicion regarding music. In *The Republic,* Plato wrote passionately about the importance of the close regulation of music and dance. While Aristotle disagreed on what the restrictions should be, he too supported close scrutiny. During the time of Euripides, restraints on public (secular) music were relaxed, "leaving the public with a music which appealed to the emotions without carrying with it any exalted connotation whatever, and without manifesting or demanding any of the discipline which in the older view was music's first need. . . . the status of the musician in Roman society was notably low" (Routley 1950: 39, 40). St. Augustine (second century C.E.) is generally credited with laying the groundwork for similar attitudes toward music in the Christian church. Later on, John Calvin (1509–1564) set forth restrictions on musical expression that guided the Puritans.

4. Kabbalists are students of the Zohar, a talmudic-era mystical work, and spiritual descendants of Palestinian rabbis Joseph Karo and Shimon Bar Yochai.

5. Hasidim perpetuate the spiritual legacy of Rabbi Israel Baal Shem-Tov (1700–1760), who believed that singing and dancing were two of the highest forms of prayer.

6. One could argue that religious orientation is a common theme in the klezmer revival, but I believe it is most often used as a postmodern sort of posture (as in John Zorn's *Tzaddik* [pious person] record label), rather than as an endorsement of any actual system of beliefs.

7. It is not clear whether this quote implies intentional or unintentional mockery, since klezmorim have certainly been no strangers to parody over the years.

8. For a detailed history of European klezmorim in the Middle Ages, see Salmen 1991.

9. The feast of Purim is the occasion for the annual chanting of the biblical book of Esther, which details how the Jews of pre-Common Era Persia are saved from annihilation by the rather unconventional deeds of a clever Jewish queen and her uncle. On that holiday, rabbis have suggested that Jews should become so intoxicated that they cannot tell the heroes from the villains.

10. The term "carnivalesque" comes from the writings of Russian literary historian Mikhail Bakhtin, who used it to characterize the earthy and unbridled nature of medieval popular culture, particularly in its expression through "popular festive forms." In Bakhtin's view, carnival is a world of "topsy-turvy, of heteroglot exuberance, of ceaseless overrunning and excess where all is mixed, hybrid, ritually degraded and defiled" (Stallybrass and White 1986: 8).

11. This is not to say that klezmer music was exclusively an oral tradition; only that notation skills were relatively rare among its less virtuosic practitioners. It has also been observed that much of the notated music that might have been handed down from earlier times was lost due to Russia's many wars (Beregovski 1982: 20). Another obvious reason for the scanty preservation of klezmer materials has been the lack of interest in such materials on the part of both Jewish and general music archives until very recently.

12. According to some accounts, Gusikov's Viennese debut was on the Jewish Sabbath (Sapoznik 1999: 4), and his final concert is rumored to have taken place on the afternoon of Yom Kippur.

13. Some of Kholodenko's elaborate concert works were published in Beregovski 2001.

14. The pay scales in klezmer *kapelyes* (bands) generally differed according to instrument, with the drummer getting the smallest share. This practice inspired the Yiddish proverb, *Er hot a vert azey vi der pukler bay di klezmer* (He is as wealthy as a klezmer drummer). The sums paid to klezmorim never amounted to a substantial income, even including the tips that were earned when requests were played (Beregovski 2001: 34).

15. A common nickname, *klezmuruk*, with its Ukrainian suffix, was applied to klezmorim by Jewish classical musicians who wanted to distance themselves from them.

16. I was personally privileged to experience old-world Hasidic attitudes toward klezmorim while performing at a wedding in the Boro Park section of Brooklyn in 1983. Since the wedding was held during the month of Adar (the coldest time of the year and a traditional time to show extra hospitality toward beggars), many beggars were present. When it came time to eat, the band—which included trumpeter Frank London, vocalist Michael Alpert, clarinetist Andy Statman, and me—was seated with the beggars and served scraps from a large trough.

17. Joshua Horowitz postulates that there were four levels of musicians in European Jewish society: established virtuosic klezmorim who relied on gifts from the nobility; Hasidic court musicians who were given regular salaries; professionals and semi-professionals who relied on tips, table money, and *tantsgeld* (a negotiated sum for each dance); and itinerants who played not only at weddings but also at fairs and street gatherings (2000, pers. comm.).

18. The practice of having klezmorim bid on and leave a deposit for the privilege of playing a wedding still goes on in contemporary Moldova (Goldenshteyn 1999).

19. For a look at unionizing activities of Jewish musicians in late nineteenth-century New York, see Loeffler 2002.

20. A complete discography of America's Eastern European–oriented Jewish ethnic recordings up to 1940 can be found in Spottswood 1990.

21. For a poignant critique of the gulf between recorded dances and live folk music, see Carson (1997: 81–86).

22. For an in-depth exploration of the lives and work of Dave Tarras and Naftule Brandwein, see Sapoznik 1999 and especially Rubin 2001.

CHAPTER 2

1. Philadelphia's tolerance of religious minorities goes back to the city's Quaker origins in 1683. Boston's less tolerant Puritans sent its first Jewish settlers back to Europe (Friedman 1983: 5). In marked contrast to New York's Sephardic (mostly Dutch Jews of Spanish descent) and German Jews, who conspicuously discouraged Eastern European Jewish immigration, Philadelphia's Jewish charities welcomed the new immigrants (in 1881) with the only welcoming celebration ever held for Jews from Eastern Europe (6).

2. A notable exception was the Lemisch family, a renowned Romanian and Galician klezmer dynasty that became established in Philadelphia possibly as early as the 1860s. Violinist Selig Itsik Lemisch was already a well-known local klezmer when he became the orchestra leader for Yiddish productions at the Thalia Theatre (located in the Northern Liberties section of the city) in 1881. He and his family orchestra were well respected by both Boris Thomashevsky and Jacob P. Adler (two major actors of the late 1800s), and he was most likely the model for the lead character in Jacob Gordin's Yiddish drama, *Selig Itsik, the Klezmer* (Boonin 1999: 54).

3. Hasidic Jews, who relied heavily on their *rebbes* (religious leaders) for interpretation of all scriptural matters, were generally less educated in the complexity of Jewish law

than their non-Hasidic Orthodox counterparts (known as *misnagdim*). This was particularly true of Hasidim from Galicia, Ukraine, and Moldova.

4. Joseph Hoffman's immigration story is worth noting. The elder Hoffman, a cornetist and violinist seeking to escape the Russian Army on the brink of the Russo-Japanese war, bought a ship's ticket to Argentina, where his relatives were waiting to receive him. Only after the boat landed did he realize that he had mistakenly gone to Philadelphia (Hoffman 1996a).

5. Bandleader Lou Lemisch was descended from violinist and Yiddish theater conductor Selig Itzik Lemisch (see note 36). The Romanian branch of the Lemisch family is still remembered by Gypsy and Romanian musicians. Violinist, filmmaker, and author Yale Strom (1996) recalled that he encountered several musicians in Iasi, Romania, who taught him "Lemisch" repertoire as recently as 1990.

6. Samuel Feldsher (1988) remembered that in Europe such allegiances were more fluid: "Teplek was a small Jewish town surrounded by non-Jewish ones. Itsikl and Grossman called themselves 'Di Broder Kapelle' because they were probably originally from Brody—it's not too far away. There was another band in Teplek; they came from a town called Darshev. We used to call them the Darshever Kapelye. Now, for example, the city Isin was a big town but they didn't have any Jewish musicians, so whenever there was a wedding the musicians from Teplek had to go to Isin."

7. Hasidic and Orthodox weddings featured many ritual dances not performed by the less observant. Men and women were not permitted to dance together and were usually separated by a *mekhitse* (makeshift wall).

8. Several musicians whom I spoke with recalled bandleaders (including my own grandfather) who used klezmerloshn, the secret klezmer argot, when dividing up the night's earnings so that they could evade challenges to their fairness, since American-born musicians had no idea what they were talking about.

9. Klezmer and Greek repertoires have many tunes in common. This may have to do with the large number of Greeks who lived and worked in certain Eastern European cities with large Jewish populations, such as Odessa (Schwartz 1996). Gypsies and Jews shared much of their musical heritage in Romania and the Bukovina, and Jewish musicians had no trouble providing dance music for Gypsy gatherings.

10. Fighting has been documented at various types of ethnic weddings, including Jewish (see Chapter 5). Jane Cowan (1990) has documented fighting as a common recurrence at the *kefi*, the male-dominated segment of the Greek pre-wedding celebration.

11. Hotels with predominantly Jewish clientele abounded in Wildwood and Atlantic City, two popular New Jersey seashore towns.

12. The alternative, the synagogue wedding, greatly increased the expense and necessitated attention to punctuality, something that could be entirely ignored when halls were used (Patten 1905: 244).

13. "Potluck" weddings made a big comeback in the Depression era (1929–1935; Hoffman 1998).

14. This is not to imply that Hoffman learned the instrument itself on the bandstand; his teacher, Isadore Raksin, was an auxiliary member of the Philadelphia Orchestra, although he did play plenty of Jewish weddings on the side. Apprentices were never invited to sit in unless their skills on their instruments were already solid.

15. Klezmer performances in private homes marked a continuation of an old European tradition. Hosting klezmer concerts and informal dances was seen as a marker of prosperity.

16. In his biography, Sholem Secunda refers to his time in Philadelphia as his "exile," his absence from the New York scene having been engineered by the jealous "dean of Jewish composers," Joseph Rumshinsky (Secunda 1982: 80–92).

17. I am also not certain how many of the ninety-three Kandel recordings listed in the Spottswood discography were actually released; certainly many are rarities among surviving 78 RPM records.

18. While recordings tell us a great deal about repertoire, they also tend to obscure performance practice. Ten-inch 78 RPM recordings, limited to three minutes in length, promote the mistaken notion that dance tunes were performed as individual pieces; we know from oral tradition that they were virtually always combined into medleys.

19. Klezmer xylophone, a relative of the popular Eastern European straw fiddle, was more common than one might think, and Hoffman received a fair amount of competition from two other Philadelphia-based klezmer xylophonist-bandleaders, Ralph Bolden and Morris Spector.

20. Two compilations of Kandel recordings have been issued on the Global Village label.

21. The attitude in Philadelphia, and in the United States in general, seemed to differ from what I noticed among veteran Jewish professional musicians from Eastern Europe and Israel, among whom "klezmer" has endured as a functional term. I noticed a change in some American attitudes after Itzhak Perlman's klezmer documentary, *In The Fiddler's House*, came out in 1996. Perlman seemed to identify himself with klezmorim, and Jewish musicians sought to identify themselves with Perlman.

22. Here "Jewish" signifies a large variety of European genres, including many Polish, Hungarian, Russian, and Greek repertoires.

23. It was not hard to get such individuals kicked out of the union since few of them followed union protocol regarding payment scales and the like.

24. For a more complete explanation of this phenomenon see Rothstein 2002.

25. Moldavian klezmorim actually have two formal classes of pranks, calling the milder ones *donkyebar* (jackass-style) and the more serious ones *Tolstoybar* (Tolstoy-style, as in embodying *War and Peace*) (Kagansky 2000).

26. These included cellist Isidore Gusikoff, principal trombonist Charles Gusikoff, and principal trumpet Saul Katzen.

27. Every musician I spoke with had a story about Joey Singer and his audacious excuses. Bobby Roberts summed them up best: "His mother died every weekend" (Roberts 1998).

28. This story had several variants. Some insisted it was actually the bride's mother who partook, while others offered up similar scenarios involving other leaders.

29. With the advent of the "talking picture" (using the new "vitaphone" technology) in 1926, many of these musicians found themselves out of work, giving rise to a "musician's" depression that predated the 1929 Depression by three years. In such a poor work climate, Jewish music became a refuge for some who found themselves suddenly unemployed.

30. Conductor Serge Koussevitsky was rumored to have offered his biographer, Moses Smith, large sums of money to hide his family's klezmer background. In the end, Smith refused the money and revealed Koussevitsky's "scandalous" origins (Nissenbaum 1980, pers. comm.).

31. "My First Goose," an autobiographical short story by Russian author Isaac Babel (1955: 72–76), graphically captures the culture shock experienced by Jewish soldiers of Weinstein's generation.

32. Here, "outside" refers to the expression used in Philadelphia to describe musicians who played weddings, bar mitzvahs, and other individually contracted musical

engagements that fell outside of the steady work contracted by theaters and orchestras. In other cities such work went by different names, for example "general business" or "G. B." in Boston, "casuals" in Los Angeles, and "club date" in New York. For a study of club-date culture and attitudes, see MacLeod 1979 and 1992.

33. The Getzen, Gorodetzer, and Alexander families included musicians and caterers, and at least three bandleaders—Dave Kantor, Dave Axelrad and, more recently, Cal Shaw— doubled as florists.

34. Philadelphia spawned particularly intricate bar mitzvah and krinsl (crowning) ceremonies, replete with several tunes composed by the local emcees; for more on this phenomenon, see Chapter 4.

35. According to Joe Borock, this practice continued until 1989 (Borock 1997b).

CHAPTER 3

1. While both Lester Lanin and Meyer Davis were from Jewish backgrounds, both were quite careful to avoid bookings where any Jewish music might be played, lest they be pigeonholed as "Jewish" bandleaders. During a 1970s appearance on the *Dick Cavett Show*, the host directly asked Lanin whether he was Jewish. He thought it over for a moment and, with a response that has since become legendary, replied, "Not necessarily" (Borock 1997b). Bobby Roberts recalls his own experience being "outed" by a Main Line (Philadelphia non-Jewish high society) family for whom he had worked on occasion. "When I was in business, every time you opened up an *Exponent* (the top Philadelphia Jewish newspaper) you'd see my ad and my picture, my full-page ad, and there was this gentile girl whose family I'd worked for once in a while. And she come to my office to book work, but then she said, 'Bobby, we all like you, but I need to look into something, I heard some rumors, let me get back to you. And later we were having lunch in the lobby at the Parkway House (a posh Center City hotel), and she said, 'We've decided we won't have your band.' And I said, 'Why not?' And she said, 'You're too Jewish. And you'll never play the Main Line again.' And I never did" (Roberts 1998).

2. Borock moved to Philadelphia from Lebanon, Pennsylvania, in his early teen years.

3. During this time period, the Uhr family also owned another catering establishment, the Wynne Ballroom, located in Wynnefield, a newer neighborhood in west Philadelphia.

4. In his study of the evolution of the bulgar Walter Zev Feldman (2002) came to a similar conclusion regarding New York's klezmer repertoire.

5. After going on to a stellar career in New York, trumpeter Mel Davis once got into serious trouble playing New York Jewish repertoire that he had learned in Philadelphia. Figuring he would impress his new employer, legendary bandleader Dave Tarras, he launched into several difficult "Tarras Freylekhs" that he remembered from the Harry Swerdlow book. Swerdlow had seldom transcribed anything from recordings, preferring to sit in the back of New York wedding halls and write tunes down as he heard them. Davis was, of course, taken aback when Tarras stared at him instead of joining in. Afterward, the master's only words were "What was that?" (Davis 1997a).

6. Boston's tradition is traced to a large number of related families all emigrating from the southern Ukrainian town of Iazaslav (Drootin 1996). Milwaukee's klezmer heritage was brought there from Riga, Latvia (Aaron 1993).

7. New York clarinetist and saxophonist Howie Leess (1998) recalls that any time he ran out of freylekhs he would defer to Mel Davis who always seemed to know plenty of extra tunes that Leess had never heard before.

8. For example, Neff was the only one of the Jewish leaders at the time who played regularly for Philadelphia's affluent German Jews.

9. Both in their eighties at the time, reedmen Leess and Pincus were two of New York's most highly respected Jewish and club-date musicians.

10. Ironically, Hoffman Watts's participation in the klezmer revival scene earned her a National Heritage Fellowship in 2007.

11. Kessler's use of the Boston term "G. B." (general business) to describe functional wedding bands marks him immediately as an outsider in the Philadelphia scene.

12. Founded in the late 1980s, the Klezmatics have set the standard for reinterpreting Eastern European Jewish music within a contemporary esthetic framework.

CHAPTER 4

1. It was and still is fairly common practice for a Jewish congregation to host a musical celebration when it receives a new Torah scroll. In Hasidic communities, these celebrations often include a parade through the streets from the house of the benefactor to the synagogue. My first paid musical engagement (in 1966, at age eleven) was such a procession, from the home of the benefactor near the corner of Vernon Road and Stenton Avenue in East Mt. Airy, down Stenton Avenue to Beth Solomon, a Hasidic synagogue on Sedgewick St., led at the time by Grand Rabbi Meyer Isaacson.

2. There are very little published data on American Jewish weddings, and of the authors who have written about the Philadelphia Jewish community, only Patten 1905 explores the subject at all. Consequently, most of the data in this chapter were gathered from personal interviews.

3. The term "liminal" was coined by Arnold Van Gennep in the early twentieth century to define "life crisis" rituals that celebrate a "change of state." As such, they involve a move from separation, the moment when individuals relinquish their previous status in the community, through a liminal phase, a time of transition, and finally into a phase of incorporation, when, in the case of a wedding, the community welcomes them back in their new state as a married couple. For a more detailed look at the history and meaning of such rituals, see Turner 1969.

4. This observation is that of Beregovski (2001), who begins his book on klezmer with a chapter on the klezmer in Jewish folklore.

5. Jane Cowan has documented a similarly close connection between the musicians and the wedding party at Greek weddings in Sohos, a small Macedonian community. Over the course of two days (usually Saturday afternoon through Sunday evening), the *daulia*, a small but raucous band composed of drums and zornas, lead the wedding party and other townspeople from the groom's house through the streets of the town, back to the groom's house, then to the home of the bride, and finally to the courtyard of the church where the ceremony takes place (Cowan 1990: 98–106).

6. The "crowning" of the bride's mother, unknown to Lithuanian Jews, Lubavitcher Hasidim, or informed observers of Jewish life in Chicago and other cities, is also traditionally observed by Ukrainian Christians (Tabak 1990: 120)

7. Patten, an outsider, was clearly unimpressed with the music of the klezmorim or other popular musicians of the time, and like a true social worker would, she longed for her charges to aspire to better taste in leisure activities. In her conclusion she writes, "A rare evening of good music echoes for months in the memories of the young men and women who almost nightly hear the clattering discords of the dance-hall. Sometimes the greatest pity and pathos of it all seems to be the fertility of the field which awaits the

seeds of Order, Beauty, and Knowledge so seldom flung within its boundaries" (1905: 248).

8. It is clear from this report that separate dancing was not uncommon in early twentieth-century Philadelphia.

9. For a thorough discussion of many issues concerning Jews and eroticism, see Biale 1988.

10. Hertzberg's observations are based on an interview with Hollywood movie producer, Dore Schary, in which he recalled his parents' catering hall, Schary Manor in Jersey City—later the likely model for the opulent wedding hall portrayed in Phillip Roth's popular novel, *Good-Bye Columbus.*

11. The wedding Patten referred to here may not have reflected immigrant tardiness, as she implied, but rather the Jewish custom of waiting until at least an hour after the end of the Jewish Sabbath to begin a traditional wedding ceremony. Such weddings routinely took place after 10 p.m. during daylight savings time. Musicians were often employed to play for long stretches preceding the ceremony even as the guests trickled in; most musicians had no qualms about performing on the Sabbath, and there was no regulation of such practices, even at kosher halls (Hoffman 1999).

12. "The prevailing notion has been that the masses of Eastern and Central European Jews who came to the United States between 1880 and 1924 were overwhelmingly Orthodox. The evidence suggests that most of the nominally Orthodox immigrants to the United States during those years possessed primarily an ethnic commitment to elements of Jewish tradition rather than a religious commitment. . . . the American life-style that the immigrants adopted did not entail a decision to opt out of traditional Judaism but rather a decision to substitute new social and religious mores for the older ones" (Shubert Spero, cited in Tabak 1990: 17). In *The Jews in America,* Arthur Hertzberg points out that European rabbis constantly preached to their constituents about the evils of the new world and that those who made the journey to the United States were often the least educated and usually nonobservant (1989: 152–162).

13. One example I found implying the existence of an earlier, fully European-style Jewish wedding music tradition in Philadelphia is the corpus of Harry Kandel, who recorded, among other traditional selections, a capsulated "old-world" wedding (cited earlier in less detail) on a twelve-inch disk in 1917. This recording, featuring Isidore Meltzer, an early radio personality, as badkhn, includes a march for the groom, a kale bezetsn (tune for serenading the bride), khusn kale mazel-tov (congratulations to the groom and bride), a Hasidic-style tish-nign (table song), and a freylekhs. Samuel Feldsher, an older immigrant from Teplek, Ukraine, whom I interviewed in 1986, described Philadelphia weddings that included badkhonim and many European customs.

14. In Philadelphia's Jewish community, Jews became acculturated among Jews—the dense ghetto of South Philadelphia simply gave way to other intensely Jewish neighborhoods, and cultural customs were quite slow to die (Tabak 1990: 420).

15. One of my informants mentioned that, until the late 1940s, rabbis also permitted weddings with music on Saturday afternoons; others have insisted that he must have been talking about bar mitzvahs.

16. Jewish tradition prohibits the groom from seeing the bride for a week prior to the wedding, but less observant Jews usually shortened the period to a day or, at the very least, to the time between their arrival at the hall and the ceremony.

17. In other cities, the wedding ceremony was often preceded by a bedeken or religious ceremony for unveiling the bride, but this practice was quite rare in Philadelphia since so few of the weddings were traditional in the religious sense.

18. Although many rabbis tried to dissuade couples from using this tune because it was written by Richard Wagner, a notorious anti-Semite, and urged them to substitute Mendelssohn's wedding march, such pleas usually fell on deaf ears.

19. "When the glass is broken and the wine is drunk, the bridal party is kissed all around amid cries of 'good luck' and the music of (a) *sher* [translated here as a 'Bulgarian quadrille']. All the guests form the wedding march round and round the hall, which terminates in the move toward the supper room" (Patten 1905: 244).

20. At religious weddings, during this interlude the marriage would traditionally be consummated sexually.

21. This practice was also noted in Patten's 1905 account: "Healths are drunk, congratulatory telegrams are read (fakes, say the critics), and the wedded pair is taken to the rabbi's corner for a last word of blessing" (Patten 1905: 245).

22. Joshua Horowitz points out that the inclusion of these genres as concert music in the klezmer revival had its roots in their context at the traditional wedding (1999, pers. comm.).

23. The replacement of the earlier Hasidic-style tish-nigunim (table songs) and Eastern European dance music selections with contemporary romantic love songs from the Yiddish stage suggests a transitional move to a more American aesthetic; the Yiddish language is retained here as a symbolic reminder of European roots.

24. For a detailed look at the rise and eventual domination of the bulgar in New York City, see Feldman 2002.

25. The first strain of this tune became the opening of "Dos kishinever shtikele" (The Kishinev Piece), the popular theme song of matinee idol and cantor Moyshe Oysher who lived in Philadelphia in the early 1920s.

26. In translating Beregovski's (2001) Russian, Michael Alpert notes that the text oscillates between past and present tense in this chapter. He speculates that Beregovski's ambivalence concerning tense indicates that Jewish music and dance traditions may not have disappeared to the extent he indicated in a previous chapter or that he had ambivalent feelings on this issue.

27. Landsmanshaft groups also adopted the rituals and symbolism of the secret fraternal orders widespread in the late nineteenth-century United States (Soyer 1997: 30).

28. It has often been suggested that the expansion of the mezinke ritual was actually initiated by photographers (Block 1998; Borock 1997b). Musician Joe Borock recalls a wedding where the leader, Bernie Berle, called not only the family up to congratulate the bride and groom but also every table in the room. "It took about an hour and it ruined the whole wedding" (Borock 1998b).

29. A similar ritual, known as the candle-lighting ceremony, was introduced at the American bar mitzvah as early as the 1930s (Hoffman 1997). In 1950s Philadelphia, this ceremony, which took place immediately before the bar mitzvah dinner, consisted of the introduction of younger siblings to the tune of "Bar Mitzvah kinder" (Bar Mitzvah Children); the eldest sister would carry a tallis (ritual prayer shawl) while the band played "Ver hot azoy shvesterl?" (Who Has Such a Sister), while if a brother held it, the band would substitute "Ver hot azoy yingele?" (Who Has Such a Boy). The parents would proceed to strains of "Kabed es avikha" (Honor the Father), and the bar mitzvah boy to "Der neyer yid" (The New Jew). Then the bar mitzvah boy would stand in front of the cake, and the parents would place the tallis on his shoulders to the tune of "Dos talesl" (The Talis), a Yiddish theater song, and the emcee might also sing "Mother Love" (a song composed by long-time Philadelphia emcee Abe Alemar). This was followed by various

family members lighting candles in order of seniority and a speech by the bar mitzvah boy. Finally, the bar mitzvah boy would blow out the candles, and the band would play a lively recessional for the entire family (Block 1999). This ceremony has spawned offshoots at other types of Jewish celebrations.

30. The full title of the song, composed by Mark Warshavsky, is "Di mezinke iz oys-gegebn" (The Youngest Daughter Is Married Off),

31. One contrast between the repertoires of Philadelphia and New York is heard in the *"Ot azoy"* section of the medley: The Philadelphia version features a second section in G minor (known by some New York musicians, but not found in Kostakowsky) and a third section in D minor, as contrasted with the D freygish third section found in Kostakowsky (1916). An offensive version of this tune's lyrics (*ot azoy, kakn afn shviger*—that's the way we defecate on the mother-in-law) is known to most Jewish wedding musicians and is actually the given title in Swerdlow 1914.

32. This tune is still known in Ukraine, but never made it into the New York mez-inke ritual (Beckerman, pers. comm.; Epstein 1999; Goldenshteyn 1999; Kagansky 1999; Musiker 1999, pers. comm.; Pincus 1999; Sokolow 1998).

33. The tune used for the Philadelphia "Patsh tants" (already found in Swerdlow 1914) seems to have been used as a *kazatzhok* (Cossack dance) in other cities.

34. The order that Block describes here was not entirely standardized. Max Mandel, a popular Philadelphia emcee for more than fifty years had a different version. He would begin with the introduction of the parents to the accompaniment of "Di mezinke oys-gegebn, then he would sing "Mekhuteyneste mayne" (a song that he would explain as a wish that the two families would now be as one). Next, he would start "The Mezinke") over and call up the youngest children in the family to place the krinsls on the heads of the mothers, then he would bring in the bride and groom, then the father of the bride would embrace the mother of the groom, the mother of the bride would embrace the father of the groom, and the band would play "Ot azoy," "Sheyne kale," and the "Patsh tants" (Watts 1955, audio recording.

35. New York musicians continued the *dobranotsh* tradition only through the 1930s, playing the "Gute nakht" found at the end of the Kostakowsky (1916) wedding folio (Becker-man 1998, pers. comm.).

CHAPTER 5

1. We can find evidence of this in Wolff Kostakowsky's *Hebrew Wedding Music Folio,* published in New York in 1916. A sher medley titled "Philadelphia Sherele" is found on pages 154–155. The opening two sections of the piece are variants on the sher that always opens the Philadelphia medley. Interestingly, in an earlier edition of this volume, the same sher medley is titled only "Sherele" and is attributed to Mr. Kostakowsky.

2. Other scholars have looked at klezmer music traditions in various communities, and Walter Zev Feldman has written a pivotal essay on the progressive development of the Romanian *Bulgareasca* (Feldman 2002: 84–126), but no one has focused exclusively on the American incarnation of the Russian Sher.

3. In several recorded versions (an Abe Schwartz 78 RPM recording, Columbia 84013, recorded February 1918, and an I. J. Hochman 78 RPM recording, Columbia 3430-3, also recorded 1918), the dance is called a "Russian Quadrille."

4. Same-sex dancing figures prominently in biblical accounts of Jewish dance (Freid-haber 1985–1986). See also http://www.angelfire.com/ns/helenwinkler/resourcepage.

5. Similar hip movements have been noted in the version of the quadrille danced in Martinique (Gerstin 2000).

6. According to clarinetist Marty Levitt (2003), a similar kind of signal (in this case, four bars taken from one of the cadential passages) was traditionally used in New York.

7. Such a promenade is a component of many Russian folk dances (Lawson 1953: 88).

8. Chain dances may have their roots in the idea of breaking a circle so that evil might leave or good might come in (Lawson 1953: 20).

9. Warsaw-born klezmer Ben Bazyler once remarked that members of the "patron's" set would routinely fight with dancers who joined in uninvited without paying (Alpert 2003, pers. comm.).

10. More recently, a great deal of discussion has emerged over the coordination of dance and music in the sher (see http://www.klezmershack.com, archives, November 17–19, 2003). In instructing dancers, Michael Alpert (2003, pers. comm.) encouraged them to fill out their phrases with "shining" when they were ready to move on and the musical phrase had not yet concluded.

11. In New York, a sher medley with twelve or so sections was in common use through the 1920s, but by the 1940s, that medley had dwindled in common practice to only four or five fixed parts (Beckerman 1998, pers. comm.; Epstein 1997; Musiker 1999, pers. comm.). Of the New York musicians I interviewed, only Marty Levitt (whose father was originally a Philadelphia klezmer) mentioned playing longer predetermined New York Russian Sher medleys through the 1950s (Levitt 2003). One can find evidence of earlier medleys by listening to the various sher recordings by the Abe Schwartz Orchestra. For example, one might start with the *Russian Quadriglia—Parts 1 and 2* (1918) and follow it up with any of Schwartz's "Russian Sher" or "Russian Scissors" recordings or with his recording of "Russian Sher #5" (Columbia 42296-2, recorded in April 1923). Codified New York sher medleys can also be found in Wolff Kostakowsky's *Hebrew Wedding Music Folio*, published in New York in 1916. Unfortunately, a comprehensive study of this material is beyond the scope of this volume.

12. Here Katz's reference to "all the sections" refers only to those sections that were current in the 1950s. When presented with another 1950s manuscript that was used by the Roberts society band, Katz was quick to dismiss it as having many of the "wrong" sections. In fact, the Roberts book seems to have relied heavily on much earlier sources, such as the 1914 Freed sheet music edition.

13. Harry Kandel emigrated to the United States in 1905 and was well acclimated to America by 1915. Since the manuscript I refer to contains only Russian and Yiddish titles, his daughter, Doris, concluded that it was from his early immigrant days or that it pre-dated his arrival in America. However, it is clear that some of the characteristic Philadelphia portions of the sher were added at a later date, since those sections are wedged in between other tunes.

14. This sher, mailed from Philadelphia to a non-Jewish former student of Lemisch who was living in Belz, Bessarabia, at the time, is preserved in a collection of Moldavian dance music published by Romanian violinist, composer, and musicologist Boris Kotliarov in 1955 (Feldman 2003, pers. comm.).

15. On the compositional logic of form in klezmer dance tunes see Beregovski (2001: 20–21; Feldman 2002: 101–111; Rubin 2001: 173–249; and Slobin 2000: 102–106).

16. Actually, a similar progression of tonalities might be found in New York Russian Shers, from D melodic minor to D harmonic minor to D fregish. The consistent use of D as the tonic in New York sher medleys may explain why Kostakowsky (whose folio was

published in New York) prints his version of the Philadelphia Sher in the key of D, even though Philadelphia musicians played it with A as its tonic.

17. Bela Bartok (1981, 1997. made some effort to classify Eastern European modal language, but focused mainly on trying to identify national (mostly Hungarian) traits of melodies (often forcing them into unconvincing pentatonic models) and to attain conclusive scientific classification of pitch systems. Karl Signell (1977) has written comprehensive essays on modal practice in Turkish classical music, but stops short of applying the same systematic rules to folk repertoire.

18. This grouping corresponds to the *Adonoy Molokh* (God is King) cantorial shtegyer (mode).

19. Cantorial scholars call this grouping *Mi Shebeyrekh* (the one who blessed), since it is commonly used in the chanting of that prayer.

20. Freygish corresponds to the tonal grouping that cantors call *Ahava Rabah* (abundant love).

21. While the melodic content of the medley derives from Eastern European modal rather than harmonic traditions, the musicians who put these medleys together in Philadelphia were using chordal accompaniments. To the western ear, some of their moves seem to imply a dominant to tonic relationship (in the case of A freygish moving to D) or the equivalent of a parallel minor to major shift in the case of A minor moving to A freygish. Thus, an initial A minor tonality gives way to A freygish (which implies A dominant 7), which eventually "resolves" to D minor. Subsequently, D minor gives way to D freygish or D major. Thus, the tonal groupings found in the Philadelphia Russian Sher medley are not in any way random and, in fact, exhibit similar tonal principles to those found in Bach's *Well Tempered Clavier* (minor followed by parallel major) and Beethoven sonatas (dominant/tonic).

22. For more on makam, see Signell 1977.

23. While much of the string-oriented European klezmer repertoire was in an A tonality, the clarinet and trumpet-centered American klezmer repertoire was almost always played in D. This fact gave rise to the nickname "D minor" that was used among American club-date musicians for the entire genre.

24. Henry Sapoznik (1999) postulates that the clarinet took over as the top klezmer instrument in America because it sounded better on recordings. One can also point to the decline of the violin as a Jewish folk instrument, its low standing in American popular music, and the popularity of the clarinet/trumpet/trombone combination as the front line in many kinds of American popular music ensembles.

25. The recording also introduces us to the sound of the Arch Street Yiddish Theatre orchestra of the time, since many of the same musicians who recorded with Kandel's orchestra were employed in the pit there and Kandel worked in the theater as music director in the late 1910s.

26. See Feldman 2002 for more on the popularity of these Jewish dance tunes.

27. This tune, also found in the 1914 Swerdlow manuscript, was recorded by Kandel's orchestra as "*A freylekhs nokh der khupe*" (A Dance after the Wedding).

28. The tune at the beginning of sher #8 may well have provided the prototype for the melody of Yiddish singer Moyshe Oysher's popular 1940s Yiddish hit, "Halevay" (It Should Only Happen).

29. Such traces can be found in the sher included in the 1960s Music Associates folio; stray sections of the older tunes turn up in the middle of the newer ones. Several of the older musicians I spoke with discredited the Music Associates folio for this reason.

30. As was noted earlier, a similar tonal move was part of the New York Russian Sher medley.

31. The first and last strains of this sher melody bear a striking resemblance to the "Meron Nigun" (also called "Abu's Courtyard"), a tune ubiquitous today among Hasidim in Israel. The actual Meron tune can also be found in Swerdlow 1914.

References

In addition to works cited in the text, this list includes those works helpful to me in other ways or works that might be of interest to the reader.

Aaron, Joe. 1993. Interview by Hankus Netsky, Milwaukee, November.

Abrahams, Israel. 1969. *Jewish Life in the Middle Ages.* New York: Atheneum. First published 1896.

Adler, Israel, and Ann Brenner. 1995. *The Study of Jewish Music: A Bibliographical Guide.* Jerusalem: Magnes Press.

Adler, Jerome. 1930–1945. "Foreign Music Collection." Bound music folio hand-copied by Jerome Adler, 80 Pages. Courtesy of Jerome Adler.

Alpert, Michael. 1990. "All My Life, a Musician." Unpublished manuscript. Microsoft Word file.

Avenary, H. 1972. "Music." In *Encyclopedia Judaica,* Vol. 12, 566–664. Jerusalem: Keter.

———. 1979. *Encounters of East and West in Music.* Tel Aviv: Tel Aviv University, Department of Musicology.

Babel, Isaac. 1955. "My First Goose." In *The Collected Stories.* Edited and translated by Walter Morrison, 72–77. New York: Criterion.

Baraka, Amiri [LeRoi Jones]. 1966. *Blues People: Black Music in White America.* New York: William Morrow.

———. 1970. *Black Music.* New York: William Morrow.

Bartok, Bela. 1981. *The Hungarian Folk Song.* Edited by Benjamin Suchoff. Albany: State University of New York Press.

———. 1997. *Studies in Ethnomusicology.* Lincoln: University of Nebraska Press.

Becker, Howard. 1963. *Outsiders: Studies in the Sociology of Deviance.* New York: Free Press.

Benny and the Vildachayas. 1997. *Get in Trouble.* (CD). Philadelphia: Ben Laden.

Beregovski, Moyshe. 1982. *Old Jewish Folk Music*. Translated and edited by Mark Slobin. Philadelphia: University of Pennsylvania Press.

———. 2001. *Jewish Instrumental Folk Music*. Translated and edited by Mark Slobin, Robert Rothstein, and Michael Alpert, with annotations by Michael Alpert and a foreword by Izaly Zemtsovsky. Syracuse, NY: Syracuse University Press.

Biale, David. 1992. *Eros and the Jews*. New York: Basic Books.

Block, Bobby. 1997. Telephone interview by Hankus Netsky, Boston and Philadelphia, June.

———. 1998. Telephone interview by Hankus Netsky, Boston and Philadelphia, October.

———. 1999. Telephone interview by Hankus Netsky, Boston and Philadelphia, September.

Block, Bobby, and the Klezmer Kings. 2000. *A Collection of Klezmer and Yiddish Heartwarming Melodies*. (CD). Mt. Laurel, NJ: Bobby Block.

Bohme, Franz Magnus. 1967. *Geschichte des Tanzes in Deutschland: Beitrag zur deutschen Sitten-, Literatur-, und Musikgeschichte*, 2 vols. Reprint of the Leipzig 1886 edition. Hildesheim: Gg Olms, Breitkopf and Hartel.

Boonin, Harry D. 1999. *The Jewish Quarter of Philadelphia: A History and Guide*. Philadelphia: Jewish Walking Tours of Philadelphia.

Borock, Jackie, and Hankus Netsky. 1999. *A Joyful Noise : The Lost Jewish Music of Philadelphia*. (VHS Video). Philadelphia: Borock Productions and The Philadelphia Jewish Archives Center.

Borock, Joe. 1996a. Interview by Hankus Netsky, Philadelphia, July.

———. 1996b. Interview by Hankus Netsky, Philadelphia, October.

———. 1997a. Interview by Hankus Netsky, Philadelphia, April.

———. 1997b. Interview by Hankus Netsky, Sainte-Agathe-des-Monts, Quebec, August.

———. 1999. Interview by Hankus Netsky, Boston and Philadelphia, September.

———. 2000. Interview by Hankus Netsky, Cherry Hill, NJ, December.

Boyarin, Jonathan, and Daniel Boyarin. 1997. *Jews and Other Differences: The New Jewish Cultural Studies*. Minneapolis: University of Minnesota Press.

Braun, Joachim. 1987. "The Unpublished Volumes of Moshe Beregovski's Jewish Musical Folklore." *Israel Studies in Musicology* 4:125–144.

Braunstein, Susan L., and Jenna Weissman Joselit, eds. 1990. *Getting Comfortable in America: The American Jewish Home, 1880–1950*. New York: Jewish Museum.

Cahan, Abraham. 1970. *Yekl and the Imported Bridegroom and Other Stories of the New York Ghetto*. New York: Dover Publications.

———. 1993. *The Rise of David Levinsky*. New York: Penguin Books.

Cantor, Elsa Freed. 2001. Interview by Hankus Netsky, Radnor, PA, July.

Cantwell, Bill. 1993. "When We Were Good." In *Transforming Tradition: Folk Music Revivals Examined*, edited by Neil Rosenberg. Urbana: University of Illinois Press.

Carson, Ciaran. 1997. *Last Night's Fun*. New York: North Point Press.

Cohen, Geraldine (Gerri Dean). 1997. Telephone interview by Hankus Netsky, Boston and Philadelphia, June.

Cohen, Judah M. 2000. "On Becoming a Reform Cantor at the Turn of the Twenty-first Century." PhD diss., Harvard University.

Cohen, Norman. 1981. *Long Steel Rail: The Railroad in American Folksong*. Urbana: University of Illinois Press.

Cowan, Jane. 1990. *Dance and the Body Politic in Northern Greece*. Princeton: Princeton University Press.

Cowdery, James R. 1990. *The Melodic Tradition of Ireland*. Kent, OH: Kent State University Press.

Davis, Harry. 2001. Interview by Hankus Netsky, Philadelphia, July.

Davis, Mel. 1997a. Telephone interview by Hankus Netsky, Boston and Fort Lauderdale, June.

———. 1997b. Telephone interview by Hankus Netsky, Boston and Fort Lauderdale, October.

Drootin, Al. 1996. Telephone interview by Hankus Netsky, Boston and Plymouth, MA, November 8.

Ellstein, Abraham, 1940. "Der Nayer Sher" [The New Sher]. (Sheet music). New York: Metro Music.

Epstein, Max. 1996. Telephone interview by Hankus Netsky, Boston and Plantation, FL, October.

———. 1997. Telephone interview by Hankus Netsky, Boston and Plantation, FL, June.

———. 1999. Telephone interview by Hankus Netsky, Plantation, FL, February.

Familant, Joe. 1981. Interview by Hankus Netsky, Mt. Holly, NJ, August.

Feldman, Walter Zev. 1998. "Klezmer Music from Galicia." Presented at Klezkanada, Sainte-Agathe-des-Monts, Quebec, August.

———. 2000. "The Four Eras of Klezmer Music." Presented at Klezkanada, Sainte-Agathe-des-Monts, Quebec, August.

———. 2001. "Klezmer Music." Presented at Klezkanada, Sainte-Agathe-des-Monts, Quebec, August.

———. 2002. "Bulgareasca/ Bulgarish/ Bulgar: The Transformation of a Klezmer Dance Genre." In *American Klezmer: Its Roots and Offshoots,* edited by Mark Slobin, 84–124. Berkeley: University of California Press.

Feldsher, Samuel. 1988. Interview by Hankus Netsky, Philadelphia, August.

Frankel, Leon. 1982. Interview by Hankus Netsky, Philadelphia, January.

———. 1988. Interview by Hankus Netsky, Philadelphia, June.

———. 1996. Interview by Hankus Netsky, Philadelphia, August.

Freed, Morris. 1914. "Sher," Celebrated Hebrew Wedding Dance. Philadelphia: Morris Freed Music.

Freedman, Berl. 1930. Jewish wedding music folio, notated by Berl Freedman. Private collection of the Nathan Freedman family, Philadelphia.

Frieden, Kenneth. 1995. *Classic Yiddish Fiction: Abromovitsh, Sholem Aleichem, and Peretz.* Albany: State University of New York Press.

Freidhaber, Zvi. 1985–1986. "The Dance with the Separating Kerchief." *Dance Research Journal* 17/2 and 18/1: 65–69.

Friedland, Lee Ellen. 1985–1986. "Tantsn Is Lebn: Dancing in Eastern European Jewish Culture." *Dance Research Journal* 17/2 and 18/1: 77–80.

Friedman, Murray, ed. 1983. *Jewish Life in Philadelphia, 1830–1940.* Philadelphia: Ishi Publications.

———. 1986. *Philadelphia Jewish Life, 1940–1985.* Philadelphia: Seth Press.

Frigyesi, Judith L. 1982–1983. "Modulation as an Integral Part of the Modal System in Jewish Music." *Musica Judaica* 5 (1): 53–71.

Fryer, Minnie. 1997. Interview by Hankus Netsky and Jackie Borock, Wyncote, PA, June.

Gerstin, Julian. 2000. "Musical Revivals and Social Movements in Contemporary Martinique: Ideology, Identity, Ambivalence." In *The African Diaspora,* edited by Ingrid Monson, 295–328. New York: Garland Publishing.

Gold, Jackie. 2000. Telephone interview by Hankus Netsky, Boston and Philadelphia, November.

Goldenshteyn, German. 1999. Interview by Hankus Netsky, Michael Alpert, and Jeffrey Wollock, Boston, July.

———. 2000. Interview by Hankus Netsky and Michael Alpert, Boston, July.

Goldin, Max. 1989. *On Musical Connections between Jews and the Neighboring Peoples of Eastern and Western Europe*. Translated and edited by Robert A. Rothstein. Amherst: University of Massachusetts Press. First published in Russian in 1983.

Gorodetzer, Harry. 1998. Telephone interview by Hankus Netsky, Newton, MA and Merion, PA, June.

Green, Archie. 1972 *Only a Miner*. Urbana: University of Illinois Press.

Greenbaum, Bernie. 1999. Telephone interview by Hankus Netsky, Wellfleet, MA and Philadelphia, June.

Greene, Victor. 1992. *A Passion for Polka*. Berkeley: University of California Press.

Hajdu, Andre, and Yaakov Mazur. 1976. *Hassidic Tunes of Dancing and Rejoicing*. (LP) FE 4209. New York: Smithsonian Folkways Records.

Hakala, Joyce E. 1997. *Memento of Finland: A Musical Legacy*. St. Paul: Pikebone Music.

Hapgood, Hutchins. 1967. *The Spirit of the Ghetto*. Edited by Moses Rischin. Cambridge, MA: Harvard University Press. First published in 1898.

Helzner, Jules. 2006. Telephone interview with Hankus Netsky, Boston and Philadelphia. December.

Hentoff, Nat, and Nat Shapiro. 1955. *Hear Me Talkin' to Ya*. New York: Rhinehart.

Herman, Lou. 1980. Interview by Hankus Netsky, Philadelphia, June.

Hertzberg, Arthur. 1989. *The Jews in America*. New York: Simon and Schuster.

Heskes, Irene. 1985. *The Resource Book of Jewish Music: A Bibliographical and Topical Guide to the Book and Journal Literature and Program Materials*. Westport, CT: Greenwood Press.

———. 1994. *Passport to Jewish Music: Its History, Traditions, and Culture*. New York: Tara Publications.

Hirshkop, Ken, and David Shepherd, eds. 2001. *Bakhtin and Cultural Theory*. Manchester: Manchester University Press.

Hochman, I. J. 1918. *Rusish Shehr und Kadril. Performed by I. J. Hochman and Orchestra. Emerson 1306: Matrix #: 3430-3. (78 RPM recording). Recorded in New York.*

———. 1997. *Der Gassen Nigun, Master of Klezmer Music—Volume 2*, New York: Global Village Music. CD 138.

Hodier, Andre. 1956. *Jazz: Its Evolution and Essence*. New York: Grove Press.

Hoffman, Joseph. 1927. Jewish wedding music folio, notated by Joseph Hoffman. Private collection of Elaine Hoffman Watts, Havertown, PA.

Hoffman, Morris. 1978. Telephone interview by Hankus Netsky, Philadelphia, June.

———. 1996a. Interview by Hankus Netsky, Philadelphia, August.

———. 1996b. Interview by Hankus Netsky, Philadelphia, October.

———. 1996c. Telephone interview by Hankus Netsky, Boston and Philadelphia, November.

———. 1997. Telephone interview by Hankus Netsky, Philadelphia, July.

———. 1998. Telephone interview by Hankus Netsky, Boston and Philadelphia, June.

———. 1999. Telephone interview by Hankus Netsky, Boston and Philadelphia, October.

———. 2000. Interview by Hankus Netsky, Philadelphia, June.

Horowitz, Joshua. 1992. "The Ahava Rabboh Cantorial Shtayger in Klezmer Music." Unpublished manuscript.

———. 2000. "The Main Klezmer Modes." Unpublished manuscript.

Idelsohn, Abraham Z. 1929 *Jewish Music in Its Historical Development*. New York: Henry Holt.

Janikian, Leon. 1990. "Armenian Music." Unpublished manuscript. Microsoft Word file.

Joselit, Jenna Weissman. 1994. *The Wonders of America*. New York: Hill and Wang.

Kagansky, Edward. 1999. Interview by Hankus Netsky, Michael Alpert, and Jeffrey Wollock, Boston, July.

———. 2000. Interview by Hankus Netsky and Michael Alpert, Boston, July.

Kammen, Jack and Joseph Kammen. 1924. *Kammen International Dance Folio # 1*, arranged by Jack Kammen and William Scher, compiled by Joseph Kammen. Brooklyn: J. and J. Kammen Music Co.

Kandel, Harry. 1910–1915. Jewish wedding music folio. Papers of Harry Kandel, Record Group 112, Supplement 39, Sheet Music Collection, YIVO Archives. New York: YIVO Institute for Jewish Research.

———. 1918. *Rusiche Shaer (Russian Dance) Part 1 and Rusiche Shaer (Russian Dance) Part 2. Performed by Kandel's Orchestra. Victor 72102: Matrix #s: 21666-4 and 21667-5. (78 RPM recording) Recorded in New York*.

———. 1991. *Master of Klezmer Music: Russian Sher*. New York: Global Village Music. CD 128.

———. 1997. *Der Gassen Nigun, Master of Klezmer Music—Volume 2*. New York: Global Village Music. CD 138.

Katz, Dr. Samuel Jr. 1980. Interview by Hankus Netsky, Merion, PA, December.

———. 1981. Interview by Hankus Netsky, Merion, PA, May.

Katz, Marvin. 1998. Interview by Hankus Netsky, Philadelphia, June.

———. 2002. Interview by Hankus Netsky, Sainte-Agathe-des-Monts, Quebec

Keil, Charles. 1966. *Urban Blues*. Chicago: University of Chicago Press.

Keil, Charles, and Angeliki V. Keil. 1992. *Polka Happiness*. Philadelphia: Temple University Press.

Kessler, Jack. 1998. Telephone interview by Hankus Netsky, Boston and Philadelphia, April.

Khevrisa. 2000. *European Klezmer Music*. Washington, D.C. Smithsonian Folkways, SFW CD 40486.

Kirshenblatt-Gimblett, Barbara, Guest Editor. 1987. "Foodways" Special Issue. *Jewish Folklore and Ethnology Review* 9 (1): 1–27.

———. 1990. "Kitchen Judaism." In *Getting Comfortable in New York: The American Jewish Home, 1880–1950*, edited by Susan L. Braunstein and Jenna Weissman Joselit. New York: Jewish Museum.

———. 1995. "Theorizing Heritage." *Ethnomusicology* 30 (1): 36–43.

———. 2002. "Sounds of Sensibility." In *American Klezmer: Its Roots and Offshoots*, edited by Mark Slobin, 129–173. Berkeley: University of California Press.

Kleeman, Janice Ellen. 1982. "The Origins and Stylistic Development of Polish American Polka Music." PhD diss., University of California, Berkeley.

Kligman, Gail. 1994. *The Wedding of the Dead: Ritual, Poetics, and Popular Culture in Transylvania*. Berkeley: University of California Press.

Klingon Klezmer. 1999. *Honey, Would You Be Meshuga Tonight?* (CD). Philadelphia: Jack Kessler.

Kodaly, Zoltan. 1960. *Hungarian Folk Music*. Budapest: Corvina.

Kofsky, Frank. 1970. *Black Nationalism and the Revolution in Music*. New York: Pathfinder.

Kornfeld, Freddie. 1996. Telephone interview by Hankus Netsky, Boston and Philadelphia, June.

Krickberg, Dieter. 1983. "On the Social Status of the Spielmann ('Folk Musician') in 17th and 18th Century Germany, Particularly in the Northwest." In *The Social Status of the*

Professional Musician from the Middle Ages to the 19th Century, edited by Walter Salmen. New York: Pendragon Press.

Kostakowsky, Wolff N. 1916. *International Hebrew Wedding Music.* Brooklyn: Nat Kostakowsky.

Kugelmass, Jack, ed. 1988. *Between Two Worlds: Ethnographic Essays on American Jewry.* Ithaca and London: Cornell University Press.

Kugelmass, Jack, and Jonathan Boyarin. 1994. *From a Ruined Garden: The Memorial Books of Polish Jewry.* Bloomington: University of Indiana Press.

Lawson, Joan 1953. *European Folk Dance.* London: Sir Isaac Pitman and Sons.

Leary, James 1990. *In Tune with Tradition: Wisconsin Folk Musical Instruments.* Cedarburg, WI: Cedarburg Cultural Center.

Leess, Howie. 1998. Telephone interview by Hankus Netsky, Boston and New York, October

Levine, Joseph A. 1981. "Toward Defining the Jewish Prayer Modes with Particular Emphasis on the Adonay Malakh Mode." *Musica Judaica* 3 (1): 13–41.

———. 1989. *Synagogue Song in America.* Crown Point, IN: White Cliffs Media.

Levitt, Marty. 2003. Interview by Hankus Netsky, Brooklyn, November.

Lifshutz, E. 1952 "Merrymakers and Jesters among Jews." *YIVO Annual of Jewish Social Science* 7: 43–69.

Loeffler, James Benjamin 1997. A Gilgul fun a Nigun: *Jewish Musicians in New York, 1881–1945.* Cambridge, MA: Harvard College Library.

———. 2002. "Di Rusishe Progresiv Muzikal Yunyon No. 1 fun Amerike: The First Klezmer Union in America." In *American Klezmer: Its Roots and Offshoots,* edited by Mark Slobin, 35–51. Berkeley: University of California Press.

Lornell, Kip, and Anne K. Rasmussen, eds. 1968. *Musics of Multicultural America: A Study of Twelve Musical Communities.* New York: Schirmer Books.

Loza, Steven. 1993. *Barrio Rhythm: Mexican American Music in Los Angeles.* Urbana: University of Illinois Press.

MacLeod, Bruce. 1979. "Music for All Occasions." PhD diss., Wesleyan University.

———. 1992. *Club Date Musicians.* Urbana: University of Illinois Press.

Manuel, Peter. 1989. "Modal Harmony." In *Yearbook for Traditional Music,* edited by Dieter Christensen. New York: International Council for Traditional Music.

Mazor, Yaakov. 1998. *The Klezmer Tradition in the Land of Israel Anthology of Music Traditions in Israel,* Volume 11, AMTI CD 9802. (CD). Jerusalem: Music Research Centre, The Hebrew University of Jerusalem.

Murray, Albert. 1976. *Stomping the Blues.* New York: McGraw-Hill.

Myerhoff, Barbara. 1980. *Number Our Days.* New York: Simon and Schuster.

Neff, Abe. Circa mid-1940s. *Russian Sher. Philadelphia: 20th Century Records. Matrix #: 2315A (78 RPM recording).*

Netsky, Hankus. 2002a. "American Klezmer: A Brief History." In *American Klezmer, Its Roots and Offshoots,* edited by Mark Slobin, 13–23. Berkeley: University of California Press.

———. 2002b "Klezmer in Jewish Philadelphia." In *American Klezmer: Its Roots and Offshoots,* edited by Mark Slobin 52–72. Berkeley: University of California Press.

Nettl, Bruno. 1983. *The Study of Ethnomusicology.* Urbana and Chicago: University of Illinois Press.

Nettl, Paul. 1923. *Old Jewish Musicians and Their Music.* Leipzig: Verlag Prague.

———. 1951. *Forgotten Musicians.* New York: Greenwood Press.

Nulman, Macy. 1975. *Concise Encyclopedia of Jewish Music.* New York: McGraw-Hill.

Orkin, Louis. 1950s. Jewish music folio, hand copied by Louis Orkin. Courtesy of Marvin Katz, Philadelphia.

Ottens, Rita, and Joel Rubin. 2003. *Klezmer-Musik*. Munich: Barenreiter.

Patten, Charlotte Kimball. 1905. "Amusements and Social Life: Philadelphia." In *The Russian Jew in the United States*, edited by Charles S. Bernheimer, 233–248. Philadelphia: John Winston.

Pena, Manuel H. 1985. *The Texas-Mexican Conjunto: History of a Working-Class Music*. Austin: University of Texas Press.

Peretz, I. L. 1947. "The Migrations of a Melody." In *Peretz*, edited by Sol Liptzin, 234–66. New York: Yiddish Scientific Institute–YIVO.

Peters, Murray. 2001. Interview by Hankus Netsky, West Palm Beach, FL, February.

Philadelphia Klezmer Heritage Ensemble. 1997. *The Lost Jewish Music of Philadelphia*. (Cassette recording). Produced by Jackie Borock and Hankus Netsky.

Pincus, Paul. 1999. Interview by Hankus Netsky, Sainte-Agathe-des-Monts, Quebec, August.

Portnoy, Joe. 1997. Interview by Hankus Netsky, Phiadelphia, June.

Portnoy, Marty. 2000. Interview by Hankus Netsky, Cherry Hill, NJ, December.

The Prophets: Nevi'im. 1978. Philadelphia: Jewish Publication Society of America.

Rabinovitsh, Sholom. 1979. "Stempeniu, a Jewish Romance." In *The Shtetl: A Creative Anthology of Jewish Life in Eastern Europe*, translated and edited by J. Neugroschel, 287–375. New York: Perigree Books.

Raksin, David. 1998. Telephone interview by Hankus Netsky, Boston and Los Angeles, March.

Rasmussen, Anne K. 1997. "The Music of Arab Detroit: A Musical Mecca in the Midwest." In *Musics of Multicultural America: A Study of Twelve Musical Communities*, edited by Kip Lornell and Anne K. Rasmussen, 73–82. New York: Schirmer Books.

Rischin, Moses, ed. 1987. *The Jews of North America*. Detroit: Wayne State University Press

Rivkind, I. 1960. *Klezmorim: Perek b'toldot ha-amanut ha-amamit* [Klezmorim: Jewish Folk Musicians: A Study in Cultural History]. Published by the author. In Hebrew.

Roberts, Bobby. 1998. Interview by Hankus Netsky, Bala Cynwyd, PA, June.

Rogovoy, Seth. 2000. *The Essential Klezmer*. Chapel Hill: Algonquin Books.

Rosenberg, Neil. 1993. *Transforming Tradition: Folk Music Revivals Examined*. Urbana: University of Illinois Press.

Roskies, David. 1998. *The Search for a Usable Jewish Past*. Bloomington: Indiana University Press.

Rothman, Doris Kandel. 1998. Telephone interview by Hankus Netsky, Boston and Philadelphia, June.

Rothstein, Robert. 2002. "Klezmer-Loshn, the Language of Jewish Folk Musicians." In *American Klezmer: Its Roots and Offshoots*, edited by Mark Slobin, 24–34. Berkeley: University of California Press.

Routley, Erik. 1950. *The Church and Music; An Enquiry into the History, the Nature, and the Scope of Christian Judgement on Music*. London: Duckworth.

Rubin, Joel. 1998. "Rumenishe Shtiklekh: Klezmer Music among the Hasidim in Contemporary Israel." *Judaism* 185 (47): 12–23.

———. 2001. "The Art of the Klezmer: Improvisation and Ornamentation in the Commercial Recordings of New York Clarinetists Naftule Breandwein and Dave Tarras 1922–1929." PhD diss., City University, London.

Salmen, Walter. 1991. *Judische Musikanten und Tanzer vom 13. Bis 20. Jahrhundert*. Innsbruck: Edition Helbling.

Sapoznik, Henry. 1981. *Klezmer Music 1910–1942: Recordings from the YIVO Archives.* (LP) FW34021. New York: Folkways Records and Service Corp.

———. 1999. *Klezmer!* New York: Schirmer Books.

Sapoznik, Henry and Pete Soklow. 1987. *The Compleat Klezmer.* Cedarhurst, NY: Tara Publications.

Scholes, Percy A. 1935. *The Puritans and Music.* London: Oxford University Press.

Schuller, Gunther. 1968. *Early Jazz: Its Roots and Musical Development.* New York: Oxford University Press.

———. 1989 *The Swing Era: The Development of Jazz, 1930–1945.* New York: Oxford University Press.

Schwartz, Abe. 1918. *Russian Quadriglia, Pt. 1, 2. Russky Norodny Orkestr (otherwise known as the Abe Schwartz Orchestra). New York: Columbia. E 3998: Matrix #: 84103 (78 RPM recording). Recorded in New York.*

———. 1920a. *Roumanian Doina. New York: Columbia. E 4825: Matrix #: 86285-2. (78 RPM recording). Recorded in New York.*

———. 1920b. "Sher, Part 1," and "Sher, Part 2." *Morris Fried [sic], Phila. PA New York: Columbia. E 4905: Matrix #s: 86691-2 and 86692-1. (78 RPM recording) Recorded in New York.*

———. 1923. *Russian Sher #5.Emerson Matrix #: 13223. (78 RPM recording). Recorded in New York.*

———. 2000. *National Hora—Master of Klezmer Music, Volume 2.* New York: Global Village Music. CD 140.

Schwartz, Martin. 1996. "Klezmer and Greek Music." Presented at Klezmer conference, Wesleyan University, October.

———. 2000. "On Connections between Klezmer and Greek Music." Presented at Klezkanada, Sainte-Agathe-des-Monts, Quebec, August.

Secunda, Victoria. 1982. *Bei Mir Bist Du Schon: The Life of Sholom Secunda.* Weston, CT: Magic Circle Press.

Sendrey, Alfred. 1969. *Music in Ancient Israel.* New York: Philosophical Library.

———. 1970. *The Music of the Jews in the Diaspora.* London: Thomas Yoseloff.

Shapiro, Jack. 1968. Philadelphia Russian Sher medley, performed by Jack Shapiro Orchestra. (Audio cassette). From private collection of Alan Shapiro, Philadelphia.

Sherr, Chick. 1997. Interview by Hankus Netsky, Philadelphia, August.

Shiloah, Amnon. 1992. *Jewish Musical Traditions.* Detroit: Wayne State University Press.

Signell, Karl. 1977. *Makam: Modal Practice in Turkish Art Music.* Seattle: Asian Music Publications/University of Washington Press.

Singer, Isaac B. 1982. *Collected Stories.* New York: Farrar Straus Giroux.

Sokolow, Pete. 1998. Interview by Hankus Netsky, Sainte-Agathe-des-Monts, Quebec, August.

Solinski, Josef. c1907–1908. *Rumänische Fantasien # 3, teil 3 [Romanian Fantasy #3]. Josef Solinski (violin), tsimblist unknown. New York: Columbia. Matrix # 124161. (78 RPM recording). Recorded in Warsaw.*

Sklare, Marshall. 1959. *The Jews.* Glencoe, IL: Free Press.

———. 1967. *Jewish Identity on the Suburban Frontier.* New York: Basic Books.

———. 1974. *The Jew in American Society.* New York: Behrman House.

Slobin, Mark. 1982. *Tenement Songs: The Popular Music of the Jewish Immigrants.* Urbana: University of Illinois Press.

———. 1989. *Chosen Voices: The Story of the American Cantorate.* Urbana: University of Illinois Press.

———. 1993. *Subcultural Sounds: Micromusics of the West*. Hanover, NH: Wesleyan University Press.

———. 1998. "Searching for the Klezmer City." Unpublished manuscript. Microsoft Word File.

———. 2000. *Fiddler on the Move: Exploring the Klezmer World*. Oxford: Oxford University Press.

———. ed., 2002. *American Klezmer: Its Roots and Offshoots*. Berkeley: University of California Press.

Soyer, Daniel. 1997. *Jewish Immigrant Associations and American Identity in New York, 1880–1939*. Cambridge, MA: Harvard University Press

Spector, Max. 1998. Telephone interview by Hankus Netsky, Boston and Philadelphia, June.

Spottswood, Richard. 1991, *Ethnic Music on Records, 1893–1942*. Urbana: University of Illinois Press.

Stallybrass, Peter, and Alon White. 1986. *The Politics and Poetics of Transgression*. Ithaca: Cornell University Press.

Strom, Yale. 1996. "My Klezmer Fieldwork in Eastern Europe." Presented at the 1996 Wesleyan Klezmer Music Research Conference, Middletown, CT.

———. 2002. *The Book of Klezmer*. Chicago: A Capella Books.

Stutschewsky, Joachim. 1959. *Ha-Klezmorim: Toldoteham, orakhhayehem, b'yezirotehem* [The Klezmorim: Their History, Folklore, and Compositions]. Jerusalem: Bialik Institute. In Hebrew.

Sugarman, Jane C. 1997. *Engendering Song: Singing and Subjectivity at Prespa Albanian Weddings*. Chicago: University of Chicago Press.

Swerdlow, Harry. 1945. Unpublished Jewish wedding music folio. Private collection of Joseph Borock, Philadelphia.

Swerdlow, Meyer. 1914. Unpublished Jewish wedding music folio. Private collection of Dr. Samuel Katz, Merion, PA.

Tabak, Robert P. 1990. *The Transformation of Jewish Identity: The Philadelphia Experience, 1919–1945*. Ann Arbor: University Microfilms.

Titon, Jeff Todd, ed. 1992. *Worlds of Music*. New York: Schirmer Books.

Turner, Victor. 1969. *The Ritual Process: Structure and Anti-Structure*. Chicago: Aldine Publishing.

Uhr, Bernie. 1998. Telephone interview by Hankus Netsky, Boston and Atlantic City, July.

———. 2000. Interview by Hankus Netsky, Cherry Hill, NJ, December.

Watts, Elaine Hoffman. 1955. Recording of her wedding. (Audio recording transferred to cassette in 2000). Courtesy of Elaine Hoffman Watts.

———. 2000. Interview by Hankus Netsky, Cherry Hill, NJ, December.

———. 2001. Interview by Hankus Netsky, Boston and Havertown, PA, June.

Watts, Elaine Hoffman, and Susan Watts. 2004. *I Remember Klezmer: The Art of Klezmer Drumming*. (CD). Philadelphia: Elaine Hoffman Watts and Susan Watts.

Weinstein, Bernie. 2007. Telephone interview by Hankus Netsky, Wellfleet, MA and Philadelphia, PA, July.

Weinstein, Jerry. 1997. Interview by Hankus Netsky, Amherst, MA, August.

Weisser, Albert. 1954. *The Modern Renaissance of Jewish Music*. New York: Bloch Publishing.

Wertheimer, Jack. 1987. *The American Synagogue: A Sanctuary Transformed*. Cambridge: Cambridge University Press.

———. 1993. *A People Divided: Judaism in Contemporary America*. New York: Basic Books.

The Writings: Kethubim. 1982. Philadelphia: Jewish Publication Society of America.

Yablonsky, Norman. 1960s. Jewish music folio compiled for Music Associates Booking Agency and hand-notated by music copyist Al Boss. Courtesy of Bobby Block, Philadelphia.

Zeft, Morris. 1981. Telephone interview by Hankus Netsky, Philadelphia, July.

Zheng, Su De San. 1993. "Immigrant Music and Transnational Discourse: Chinese American Music Culture in New York City." PhD diss., Wesleyan University.

Zipperstein, Steven J. 1986. *The Jews of Odessa: A Cultural History 1794–1881.* Stanford, CA: Stanford University Press.

Index

Page numbers in italics refer to figures.

Hankus Netsky is Chair of Contemporary Improvisation and Director of the Jewish music ensemble at the New England Conservatory in Boston. He is also the Founder and Director of the Klezmer Conservatory Band, an internationally renowned Yiddish music ensemble. He has collaborated, performed, and recorded with many well-known artists, including Itzhak Perlman and Theodore Bikel.